M E R I C A

U N I T E

STATES

Washin

Charlestown

New Orleans

GULF OF MEXICO

MEXICO

S.Lucas

Socoro

Mexico

CUBA

Jamaica   Domingo

CARIBBEAN SEA

Guatimala

GUATIMALA

Caraccas   Trinadad

Bay of Panama   St.Fe   COLOMBIA   GUIANA

Galapagos

G. of Guayaquil   R. Amazon or Maranon

C.Blanco   SOUT

Lima   PERU

AMER

Easter I.   S.Felix   CHILI   Rio Jar

Valparaiso   Buenos Ayres   R. de

Juan Fernandez I.

Valdivia   G. of St.Anto

Chiloe

EAST   WEST VARIATION   VAR

T0041506

Praise for *Rum Rebels*

"Maggie Campbell, Karen Hoskin, and Joy Spence are three of my favorite master blenders. Reading their stories of adversity faced and overcome, told in their own words in Rum Rebels, left me admiring them even more."

—Jeffrey "Beachbum" Berry

"Girls and women can do anything with the right education and support, and having strong female role models in the spirits industry and beyond is key. Representation is important! A book like Rum Rebels gives you a sneak peek into this world."

—Lorena Vasquez, master blender of Zacapa

"Anyone facing uncertainty or difficulty in their own career path will be inspired by the stories of these remarkable women, who rose above their struggles and doubts to be recognized as masters of their craft. I particularly love that Halas and van Hoven have included a cocktail recipe from each of the women featured, giving us all the opportunity to share a drink with them in spirit and toast to their success."

—Katie Stryjewski, author of Cocktails, Mocktails, and Garnishes from the Garden

Rum Rebels

A Celebration of Women Revolutionizing
the Spirits Industry, with Cocktail Recipes

by Martyna Halas and René van Hoven

yellow pear press

CORAL GABLES

Cover Design & Art Direction: Elina Diaz
Cover Photo/Illustration: Adobe Stock (Queen, The Len)
Interior Photo/Illustration: Adobe Stock (Bill81, RTimages)
Layout & Design: Katia Mena

For permission requests, please contact the publisher at:
Mango Publishing Group
2850 S Douglas Road, 4th Floor
Coral Gables, FL 33134 USA
info@mango.bz

For special orders, quantity sales, course adoptions and corporate sales, please email the publisher at sales@mango.bz. For trade and wholesale sales, please contact Ingram Publisher Services at customer.service@ingramcontent.com or +1.800.509.4887.

Rum Rebels: A Celebration of Women Revolutionizing the Spirits Industry, with Cocktail Recipes

Library of Congress Cataloging-in-Publication number: 2021951257
ISBN: (print) 978-1-64250-731-7, (ebook) 978-1-64250-732-4
BISAC category code CKB041000, COOKING / History

Printed in the United States of America

Contents

Foreword
by Liz Palmer

Rum—historically considered a man's drink—surprisingly has some female roots and distillers. Rum has also been a male-dominated industry, but as you will see, women are catching up!

You will find plenty of books about whiskey in the marketplace, but finding books focused on rum are comparatively few and far between. Of the ones I did manage to find, the topics included: how to drink rum, classic rums, new-generation rums, rhum agricole, premium aged rums, international rums, and rum cocktails, but never has there been a book published on global women rum distillers, until now!

For the record, there are currently almost thirty international female rum distillers, and this number is increasing on a yearly basis.

Martyna Halas and René van Hoven have researched and interviewed sixteen amazing women for this book. They are truly "Female Disruptors" who are shaking up the rum industry. You will learn how they got there and how they survived through their wonderful stories, along with some genuine historical importance from their countries. Martyna and René go right into the heart and soul of each of these extraordinary women. The book also contains some fascinating historical anecdotes and short snippets of rum production through the chapters.

I am deeply honored to write the foreword to this book. I met René van Hoven in South Africa over ten years ago while I was judging a wine-spirits competition and we hit it off. It was there that I learned of his ultimate passion for rum. René had captivated me, not only with his in-depth, historical knowledge of rum, but also with his fascinating insight into the art of rum and the styles for each country. René has earned a formidable international reputation as a spirits writer, judge, and a director of the European Network of Spirit Experts, and who happens to be one of the few rum writers in the world and one of the most respected independent authorities on rum globally. I also met the lovely Martyna Halas in South Africa three years ago, where she described the outline of the book. I encouraged her to keep at it and not to give up. I am absolutely thrilled to be part of their journey!

There has never been a better time to release this book! I'm a very strong advocate for women in the wine and spirits industry and I am very happy to say that in this male-dominated space, times are changing. Women in the industry are spawning dialogue about representation and inclusivity. We are now seeing more female distillers, founders, and CEOs. The interest in rum and the cocktail culture has reshaped the beverage industry.

Rum Rebels is the logical portable extension of a self-guided tour into the lives of these fearless women. René and Martyna have combined their extraordinary talents to give us a unique insight into women rum distillers, so pour yourself a glass of rum and sip and savor the contents of this captivating book!

Lastly, to my fellow sailors:

May your anchor be tight,
Your cork be loose,
Your rum be spiced
And your compass be true

You can't control the wind
But you can adjust your sails

Home is where the anchor drops

Sailors tell stories, pirates make legends

Liz Palmer
Multi-award-winning wine journalist, author, and influencer

Introduction

"Because I am a woman, I must make unusual efforts to succeed. If I fail, no one will say, 'She doesn't have what it takes.' They will say, 'Women don't have what it takes.'"

—Clare Boothe Luce, American playwright

Given the biological fact that women have a better sense of taste than men (we'll go more into this later), it surprises us that there are still relatively few female master blenders in the world of spirits. The women you're about to meet are the true *Rum Rebels*: living their truth despite various roadblocks, revolutionizing our palates with their delicious rums, and bringing more finesse and sophistication to a seemingly male drink. But before we dive right into their inspiring stories, let us quickly introduce ourselves (Martyna Halas and René van Hoven).

At the tender age of eighteen, René attended a party where he got served a watery Cuba Libre. It turned out the rum bottle was filled with water as it was put aside for watering plants—a fact that went unnoticed in the middle of half-drunken birthday celebrations. This sparked René's curiosity about smell and taste. He went on to study food and beverage (F&B) management, and became a chef and F&B teacher. From there, he redirected his specialty toward spirits—in particular, vintage rum, which he started collecting in his early twenties. Nowadays, he is a recurrent judge at various spirits and wine events and a bit of a rock star among rum nerds.

Following his nose and his passion for rum, he traveled to Guatemala, where he met Lorena Vasquez, the master blender of Zacapa. The result of this trip was his first book, *Journey to Above the Clouds*, which documents the company's production process and its aging facilities. Many years later, when discussing the possibility of refreshing and rewriting this book with Martyna, both asked themselves the question: how many more women out there make rum?

A wooden plaque greets visitors at Zacapa's aging facility, called The House Above the Clouds. Located in the Guatemalan mountains, the facility is 2,300 meters above the sea.

When Martyna (an actual rock star, as she's a metal front lady and touring musician) first met René, she was a total rum novice, although she already knew she had a more sensitive palate than others. When she lived in Ireland, she once ordered a Guinness at a local pub, stressing that she wanted a bottle standing on the shelf—not a cold pint and not a refrigerated can, either. After numerous protests from the bartender, she explained she preferred stouts served at room temperature due to the flavor—and he replied that he had never seen a woman ordering a "man's drink" before with such strong opinions.

Later, René would teach Martyna all about tasting, confirming her instincts that lower temperature makes the flavor disappear. Together, they traveled to several spirits festivals and tasted many old bottlings from before and after World War II, relishing in their fruity, woody, or tarry flavors.

Whereas René often dives into the technical part of the product, Martyna grew more interested in its feminine side (or lack thereof). As soon as they started researching, they found many other women making fantastic rum across the world. And as they got to know them, they understood they didn't want to write yet another technical rum book. They wanted to write about the women creators who exude extraordinary craft and dedication to this noble spirit.

We took the virtual journey through the snowy mountains of Colorado, through the vibrant streets of Cuba, to the luscious forests of Brazil to bring you this unique book. The women we spoke with lead some of the biggest rum brands and smaller craft distilleries that positively impact the world. They often had a rocky road to success, but fearless as they are, they never gave up.

Of course, we couldn't pass on the opportunity to ask our Rum Rebels about their favorite cocktails—it is a rum book, after all! Ambitious as we are, we decided to recreate them all in Amsterdam, the Netherlands, where we are based. This task would be impossible without Kayla Cross, an awesome mixologist and owner of The Little White Bird bar in Amsterdam. Not only did she help us bring our ideas to life, but she also gave the cocktails her own twist and offered insider tips to help our readers follow the recipes no matter where they may be.

At the end of the 1990s, only three female master blenders were officially recognized in the spirits industry: Joy Spence of Appleton was the first one, Lorena Vasquez of Zacapa was the second, and a third we were unable to find. We interviewed sixteen female master blenders for this book; perhaps that mysterious number three is amongst them? If any of our readers could help us solve this riddle, feel free to drop us a line at hello@tripsandtaste.com.

We also know there are others out there, and we are confident that there will be many more female rum producers as the industry continues to open its doors to women. If we left any women master blenders out, shoot us an email. We look forward to hearing their stories.

We hope these fantastic women will touch your hearts, just as they touched ours. Whether you're a seasoned rum specialist or just dipping your toes for the first time, we're confident you'll enjoy learning about their journey, legacy, and heritage the spirit carries. You'll not only learn about rum from the women that make it, but you'll also find the perfect cocktail pairing as advised by the gustatory geniuses.

But before we get there, we must cover some things.

The Better Taster

Here, we discuss biological differences between men and women. We do not mean to exclude nonbinary people; we simply focus on the available research conducted on biological males and females.

We have a question for you, dear readers, that needs to be thought over carefully. Who in the stone age would you think benefitted the most from having a better sense of smell and taste?

A. The hunter
B. The cook

In general, naturally occurring foods that taste and smell bad also happen to be bad for us. Mother Nature is warning us, and therefore, it's beneficial to be good at identifying the wrong foods. Being able to categorize and recall various scents and tastes is sometimes even life-saving. A hunter only needs to be good at catching prey and not getting killed in the process. The cook, however, needs to tell if the food is fresh, rotten, or poisonous. In addition, the cook has to gather plants, fruits, and seeds, which also require well-developed senses. So, if your answer is B (the cook)—congratulations, you're right!

Prehistoric rock paintings found in Tassili N'Ajjer, Algeria from 6000 BC

Let's continue with some classic stereotypes: the hunter was typically a man while the cook was traditionally a woman (in some tribes, women were hunters as well, but for the sake of our argument, let's focus on the general picture). This would suggest that if both genders stayed in that role for many millennia, men would get better at hunting while women would get better at smelling and tasting. From an evolutionary point of view, ancestral mothers had to detect and avoid contaminated foods and toxins, thereby protecting their fetuses, children, and partner. While these roles may not necessarily be true today, women's taste buds are still biologically more evolved than men's.

In a nutshell, women are better equipped to be alcohol tasters simply because evolution made them that way. But for the bigger and more conclusive picture (or plain fun), let's add a few more scientific facts to the cocktail.

When we say *taste*, we don't mean the kind of taste that tells you what shoes to wear or what color your shirt should be; we refer to your physical ability to recognize flavors in foods, drinks, or cosmetics. Go to any industry that needs a good taste or "nose," and you will mostly find men in charge. There are exceptions to the rule, like Madame Coco

Chanel or Estée Lauder, but the balance between men and women is not what it should be according to science.

While saying that all women have a superior sense of smell or that all men are worse at it may not necessarily be true, there are some competencies where women usually outshine their male colleagues (and some that prove the opposite). For instance, recent research shows that women tend to be better at inspirational leadership, conflict resolution, and emotional self-awareness. Tasting is another skill that generally comes more easily to women—not because a few people feel that way, but because science supports this claim. Below we'll show you the tip of the taste iceberg, with nature and nurture as a guideline.

Nature and Nurture

Let's start with a plain, dry, and female-positive fact. Several universities discovered that women have, on average, 43 percent more brain cells in the region that is responsible for the sense of smell (otherwise known as the olfactory bulb).[1] That's quite an advantage. One theory is that it helps the mother and child bond after birth; other researchers claim it's necessary for the selection of potential mates. We know for sure that it's a handy trait to have when blending rum.

The significant olfactory distinction between sexes is why women and men tend to experience tastes differently. This fact is already evident in small children of four or five years of age. Various tests have shown that young girls are generally better at identifying the natural scent of a sibling.[2] There are almost no new cells or neurons developing in adulthood, so the advanced smelling and tasting ability stays with women through all stages of life. Women are simply born with it.

---

1 Source: https://www.medicalnewstoday.com/articles/284991
2 Source: https://www.psychmechanics.com/do-women-have-strong-sense-of-smell

Research also shows that young girls tend to better recognize sweet and sour tastes than boys their age. The study determined that boys needed food to be at least 10 percent more sour or 20 percent more sweet to achieve the same taste-detection levels as girls.

When women reach childbearing age, their tasting ability is almost at its highest and reaches its peak during pregnancy. Due to heightened estrogen levels, expecting mothers are extra sensitive to intense aromas. Pregnant women's intolerance for strong odors and bitter tastes is nature's way of saying, "Stay alert to protect your baby." In terms of evolution, this makes a lot of sense. There are simply far more women needed than men to ensure the survival of our species.

Now, let's look at nurture. Nurture refers to the skills we can learn and master later in life, even if we aren't naturally born with them. Is there a way to perfect what is already there? In some cases, yes.

While certain senses don't get better the more you use them (like your vision), your sense of smell can improve with practice. In other words, you can enhance your nosing skills by expanding your brain's aroma library and learning to recognize different scents. And while women have naturally sharp smelling and tasting abilities, taste can only be further developed through practice and exposure to different foods and drinks.

When it comes to identifying flavors, women tend to use more creative language, too. They are better at distinguishing subtle nuances and can develop more fitting descriptors for the finer flavors. However, with proper training, men can catch up and become excellent tasters as well. It's just that, biologically, women have a head start, and it's up to them to nurture and develop this ability or not.

Supertasters

Does this mean that women are supertasters by default? Not necessarily. This is something that can't be practiced, either. You either are one, or you aren't. But what are supertasters, exactly?

Supertasters are extra sensitive to flavors because they have more receptors (taste buds) than an average person their size. If you have fewer taste buds, you are on the opposite side of the spectrum (a non-taster). Thus, when a supertaster and a non-taster drink the same tea with the same amount of sugar, they perceive it differently. For instance, the supertaster will say it's too sweet, while the non-taster might call it not sweet enough. This may sound contradictory as it shows that taste can't be argued. After all, two people can have polarizing opinions on the same topic, and both could be right. With the available taste buds people naturally have, they receive as much tasting information as they can. So, when tasters detect an element like sugar, the conclusion will depend on how many receptors the mouth has. And as biology tells us, men generally need a more concentrated flavor to detect taste as accurately as women.

Only 25 percent of the population[3] consists of supertasters who are highly sensitive to certain bittering compounds, just like pregnant women. Such people carry a double copy of a gene, making them extra vigilant in noticing saltiness, bitterness, and sweetness. On the other hand, non-tasters (also about 25 percent of the population) generally won't complain as much about their food since, to them, flavors are less... well, flavorful. Putting this information in the context of women versus men, around 35 percent of all women are supertasters, compared to only 15 percent of all men.[4]

---

3 Source: https://www.nidcd.nih.gov/health/statistics/statistics-taste
4 Source: https://pubmed.ncbi.nlm.nih.gov/7878086

Interestingly, Caucasian males are the group least likely to be supertasters, and people of Asian ethnicity are most likely to be supertasters.[5]

So, if women are proven to be better tasters in general, why is the male still in control of the spirits industry? It's time for a female revolution, and the rebels in this book are in the front row. But first, let's dig a little deeper into what being a master blender actually involves and why excellent tasting skills are so important for this job.

Master Blenders

Many who have heard of the term "master blender" (or "master of rum," depending on the region) often don't realize the diversity of this role. In general, a master blender, or MB, has to ensure that each product that leaves the distillery tastes precisely the same as the version made months, years, or even decades earlier. So, whenever you buy Appleton Estate at eight years old, it should taste like the bottle you purchased a year ago. To achieve this consistency, the MB (in Appleton's case, Joy Spence) needs to check the quality of the distillates, oversee the aging process, and blend several barrels of rum.

Each barrel creates a slightly different rum, and by mixing the right liquids in the right amounts, the desired taste profile is created. This may sound easy, but it's a complex task and a huge responsibility. MBs often need expert chemistry backgrounds, outstanding sensory skills, and years of training before they are ready to do this job. Not only do they need to know everything there is to know about rum, but they also need to understand the aging process and predict how the liquid will behave.

---

5   Source: https://www.nottingham.ac.uk/news/new-study-reveals-taste-is-connected-to-ethnicity-and-gender

Oftentimes, an MB must maintain the company's centuries-long legacy, and sometimes, only a family member can hold that responsibility.

As the term master blender is so broad, the exact job description will differ between distilleries. For instance, contrary to popular belief, not all MBs do the distilling themselves, as many bigger companies will have a dedicated master distiller (MD). On the other hand, some MBs are responsible for the entire operations in their company, which means they have to oversee the production process from fermenting to distilling, aging, blending, and even bottling. Typically, the bigger the distillery, the fewer smaller hands-on tasks an MB will have. That doesn't mean they have fewer responsibilities or less to do. Still, they are responsible for managing their teams, delegating tasks accordingly, and ensuring that the final product meets the desired quality standards.

To help our readers navigate through these terms, here are the four different types of MBs you will see throughout the book, which we choose to refer to as master blenders for consistency (even if the exact job title differs):

MBs Who Blend the Rum They Distill Themselves

The MB who also distills the rum is usually the owner of the entire distillery. They must be able to multitask. As they don't produce the amounts of rum that the big producers do, they're usually called craft or micro-distilleries. Karen Hoskin of Montanya Distillers is a perfect example.

MBs Who Work Closely with a Master Distiller (MD)

This type of MB may oversee the distillation process and perform quality checks, but the job itself is handed over to the master distiller (MD). Everything produced by the MD gets checked by the MB. This scenario is common in many bigger distilleries, and some of the companies often have an entire blending team led by one MB (such as Angostura).

MBs Who Outsource Spirits Production to Their Own Specifications

This scenario is like the one above, except the company doesn't distill its own alcohol for various reasons. The MB typically works with rum outsourced from another distillery. Its production still needs to follow specific requirements, so the MB communicates closely with the distillers. The MB typically completes the aging process in her company's facilities to ensure that the final product is of the highest quality. Carúpano is an example of a rum manufacturer that operates on this basis.

MBs Who Purchase Select Barrels from Other Producers

Finally, we have a rare scenario where an MB chooses rum barrels from several producers without getting involved with the distilling process. This is known as a "private label" and is common in the whisky world. The MB can only buy what is already made—and usually also aged—but she can still create new blends. Such a product isn't meant to be consistent all the time; it's supposed to be the best available at that given moment. While large producers go for a singular taste profile for each product, a private label goes for diversity. They often don't even need to blend the rum at all, but it's often necessary as the supply is limited. Chantal Comte is the only one in this book who does this, and as far as we know, she remains the only independent female rum bottler.

Although the alcohol industry and the prestigious MB title are historically associated with men, women have revolutionized rum against all odds. Here's how it all started.

Chapter 1

Rebels Through Time

Alcohol is a product created by Mother Nature and has existed long
before humankind set foot on this planet. All it needs is sugar (fruit will
do just fine) and yeast (abundantly found in the air all around us). Give
the fruit some time and warmth, and automatically, the yeast will break
down the sugar into alcohol and carbon dioxide (which you can see as
bubbles in champagne). Alcohol is that simple. Did the first sip of alcohol
taste good compared to today's standards? We highly doubt that.

In ancient times, it seems, alcohol carried greater secrets than an awful
headache the next day. The chemical process behind it remained a
mystery for some time, but the outcome was surely noticed immediately.
When alcohol production became common knowledge, it was women,
not men, who first worked on it. Men were busy hunting while women
were taking care of the children and their household. As alcohol was
seasonal and closely connected to the land, women made it from day
one, while men only enjoyed drinking it.

In 1200 BC, Mesopotamian civilization invented distillation, which, in a
nutshell, is a process of purifying a liquid through heating and cooling.
We know this because historians discovered a cuneiform tablet (a logo-
syllabic script) between the Euphrates and Tigris Rivers (in present-
day Iraq). The tablet told of a perfume maker and first known distiller,
Tapputi-Belatekallim, who mixed flowers, oils, and balsams, then added
water or other solvents and distilled the mixture. This tablet, now in

the Metropolitan Museum in New York, also contains the first indirect reference to a still. Oh, and by the way: Tapputi was a woman.

Female chemist Tapputi-Belatekallim (right) is referenced in a clay cuneiform tablet from 1200 BCE (left).

Later, the religious Greek and Roman empires regulated women and alcohol—a theme that would return over and over through time. Several religions, including Christianity, forbade women from drinking alcohol altogether. Women who tried their hand at distilling (considered a form of alchemy) were deemed witches—and burned to death.

In the days of yore, a woman on her period wasn't allowed near distilling facilities (a harmful belief that's still prevalent in some cultures). At the time, it was "common knowledge" that menstruation would somehow prevent alcohol from fermenting. Some even believed that the presence of a menstruating woman would spoil the food.

Meanwhile, Chinese and Middle Eastern cultures had found a way to increase the alcohol percentage of their wines and, subsequently, make the drink last longer. When that technique reached Europe, the church confiscated this knowledge, and only holy men could reproduce it.

Monks tried to use this technique to make *aqua vitae*, the water of life.
While they did succeed in producing and refining distilled spirits, they
never found a formula that would grant the drinker eternal life.

Finally, after several centuries of trials and errors, distilling became
more readily available to the wealthy elite. But because distilling was
expensive to perform, alcohol stayed a luxury product for a long time,
and primarily, only rich men would drink it. The lower classes had to
wait several centuries before they could taste spirits, although wine was
relatively available.

Artist's representation of distillation apparatus for *aqua vitae* by Hieronymus Brunschwig, 1512.

With the growth and acceptance of science in the seventeenth century,
women slowly returned to distilling. Finally, the witch-hunt was over,
and they began doing what our ancestral mothers had done: producing
alcohol. Of course, women still had a few restrictions.

Let There Be Rum

Let's bring rum into the story! While many people think sugarcane belongs to the Caribbean and the Americas, it originated in Asia. The Philippines and Indonesia were among the first areas where sugarcane was found. Thousands of years ago, the local Malay people on Sumatra produced a drink out of sugarcane called *brum*. Globetrotters like the Venetian explorer Marco Polo brought the cane to Europe, where it was transferred to ships and sent to the New World. This is where and when our rum story begins.

As history tells us, Christopher Columbus sailed west in 1492 and happened upon the Americas. On his second journey in 1493, he stopped by the island of Madeira (in Portugal) to meet his lover. Here, he collected some sugarcane and brought it across the Atlantic Ocean. Still, even in a total of four trips to the west, Columbus never saw the mainland. He only managed to reach several islands, now all prominent rum producers.

Around that time, sugar was more valuable than gold, and it even became the means to pay for goods. This is the main reason why planting sugarcane on newly discovered lands was so important. But of course, with sugar came an interesting byproduct. To make sugar, one needs to extract the crystals from the cane. This is done by extracting its juice, then boiling and crystallizing it. After taking out the sugar, a heavy dark syrup called molasses is left behind. This sticky mess was considered waste back then, but it still contained some of the un-crystallizable sugars. It was then given to slaves, who learned that they could do great things with this cast-off ingredient.

By adding water to molasses, slaves discovered that they could create a pleasantly sweet drink. One day, someone must have let that diluted drink stand too long in the heat, leading to natural fermentation and the creation of low-alcohol sugarcane wine, which is the basis of rum.

In the sixteenth century, a distilled drink created from this wine was called aguardente de cana (in Portuguese) or aguardiente de caña (in Spanish).

As time went by, distillation techniques evolved. Variations of the aguardente de cana are still produced in the Americas. In Brazil, the spirit is now known as cachaça, and you will likely come across many names for it in other parts of the world.

The first official distillation of the drink we call rum took place in the seventeenth century in the Caribbean. A document from Barbados, dated 1651, stated:

The chief fuddling they make in the island is rumbullion, alias Kill-Devil, and this is made of sugar canes distilled, a hot, hellish, and terrible liquor.

History books tell us that Barbados obtained distilling techniques from the Dutch who fled Brazil due to religious and political issues. Archeologists also discovered a tin bottle containing rum on the Swedish warship Vasa, which sank in 1628. Alas, the true origins of this bottle continue to remain a mystery.

With the techniques and, therefore, quality of rum growing, so did its reputation and inevitable value. At some point, rum was used to buy newly arrived slaves from Africa. Those slaves would then harvest cane in the fields, which was used to make more rum. This system created a genuinely vicious cycle known today as the slave triangle, a dark page in the history of humankind.

Slowly, the cane spirit became more prestigious, and as a result, its popularity continued to rise for decades to come. History tells us that the first American President George Washington insisted on having a barrel of Barbados rum at his 1789 inauguration. We can also assume that once established on the Caribbean islands, sugar production increased rapidly. Alcohol consumption also went up, especially when water was unsafe to drink.

With the increased wealth of most economies in Europe and the Americas came a corresponding increase in the general consumption of rum. Rum remained a luxury, but once people could afford it, the demand for it rose rapidly. In the mid-nineteenth century, alcohol intake almost doubled, resulting in the need for regulations.[6]

> Estimations state that the average adult North American in the eighteenth century drank fourteen liters of alcohol per year.

The Original Rum Rebels (No, Not the Pirates!)

In the United States, women enjoyed "intoxicating liquors" decades before they were abolished, just not in public. A lady with a drink was a sight to behold only in private, but slowly it became an accepted element of public society.

Yet in 1919, the eighteenth amendment was passed, and alcohol became illegal until 1933. The forbidden fruit tastes the sweetest, so unsurprisingly, alcohol consumption eventually increased by

---

6   Source: "Spirited Republic: Alcohol in American History," The National Archives Museum

about 70 percent during prohibition.[7] Those who could afford it kept
spending money on drinks, while a group of clandestine distillers,
called bootleggers, did their best to earn money by making alcohol.
The recession was flourishing like never before, and beggars can't
be choosers. After all, it got them closer to a product they were so
desperate to have.

Men produced, sold, and drank booze during the alcohol embargo like
never before, but who would have suspected that "ladies" would do
the same? By law, US police officers couldn't perform a body search on
women, making them ideal candidates for smugglers. With gangsters like
Al Capone in our collective memory, not many realize that there were
plenty of women in this lucrative business as well. At one point, female
bootleggers outnumbered their male colleagues five to one.[8]

Women would eventually take on the jobs that had been exclusively
reserved for men. They also started consuming more alcohol than
ever before, though the circumstances forced them to do so secretly.
There will always be discussions about its pros and cons, but the fact
remains that women's public, private, and political lives changed forever
during prohibition.

Speakeasies (private hidden nightclubs) sprang up like mushrooms
after rain; these establishments welcomed women with open arms.
It was good if men would buy drinks; it was better if women would
come along.

A happy couple would spend more dollars together than they would
as individuals (although, of course, not all men would arrive with
their wives). For bartenders, that didn't matter; if there were women
in the bar, they were likely to make a profit.

---

7 Source: https://www.jstor.org/stable/2006862
8 Source: https://www.alcoholproblemsandsolutions.org/women-bootleggers-during-prohibition-
   there-were-many

With men getting arrested every now and then, women began running their speakeasies—and adding a female touch. Apart from pouring homemade or illegally imported liquor, they served good food, curated inviting interiors, and even added a phonograph for some dancing. As their hair and dresses got shorter, women felt more liberated to enjoy themselves. They broke both the custom and the law, preparing society for the upcoming rebellion.

Two armed female bootleggers pose circa 1921

History changed the public and political life drastically for women, and their private lives underwent a serious metamorphosis. The roaring twenties were the start of rising consumerism, new technology, and uncharted territory. Advanced printing technology made catalogs and magazines of better quality, and advertising companies began targeting women as a specific group. Women were the ones who still did most of the shopping, and at the same time, they gained more ability to make their own buying choices.

Newspaper announces the end of Prohibition. No discernible women pictured.

It wasn't long until women stepped into the workforce to make their own money. In the 1940s, men were away fighting on the other side of the Atlantic Ocean; this period helped women gain more rights and liberties. The absence of men changed the way women were viewed by themselves and others while also expanding their roles within society. Women proved they had become major players in this progressive, consumer-driven culture.

The New Rum Pages

After WWII, alcohol consumption was often still a taboo for women. A US Supreme Court ruling from 1948 prohibited women from visiting bars in cities bigger than 50,000 people, a ruling that remained for more than two decades. For years, the only time you would see a woman near alcohol was on billboards or TV ads. Then, the increase of wages in the 1960s made alcohol more accessible, and although the growing economies made everything more expensive, booze stayed relatively cheap. Its popularity grew, and in the late '60s, it wasn't a novelty anymore to see women drink in public places.

With the explosion of "flower power" and the subsequent sexual emancipation, women started to increasingly pursue more "serious" jobs. Those who wanted to climb the ladder paved it for later generations, and by the '70s and '80s, women could get lucrative positions previously reserved for men. Girls also grew more interested in studying technical fields at universities, opening their doors to more career choices. Women proved they had at least the same capabilities as men.

One thing that women were naturally better at was their ability to accurately identify ingredients through smell. Although the perfume industry already had plenty of women creating delicious scents, the late '80s gave women the opportunity to show that they were also great tasters. Biology and science showed that women were simply better equipped than men to taste.[9] Men had kept women out of the distilleries for too long; it was time to conquer that fortress. It was only a matter of time before women would return to distilling and gain recognition as master blenders. Unthinkable for those who had physically lived in the earlier centuries, ridiculous for those still stuck in that era mentally. As the women in this book illuminate, we are now ready for the next stage in the history of rum.

In 1997, Joy Spence became the first woman officially appointed as a master blender in a renowned distillery. Since then, many more women have followed suit, but it wasn't a change that happened overnight. It took a lot of strength and perseverance to shake the status quo and write new pages of history. Let's open a new chapter together.

---

9   Source: https://www.psychmechanics.com/do-women-have-strong-sense-of-smell

Chapter 2

Joy Spence, Appleton Estate, Jamaica

Everyone who has met Joy, the master blender of Appleton Estate in Jamaica, remembers her infectious smile and bubbly personality. She lights up every room and brings happiness to the people surrounding her, a quality that her adoptive mother first noticed when she held little Joy in her arms. "My mother said I brought joy to her heart the moment she saw me, which is where my name came from," she tells us.

Joy grew up to be an attentive student with a keen interest in chemistry. "I owe it to my wonderful teacher, Eldora Mills, who became like my second mom to me. She taught me all about chemistry and practical lab skills. She was also looking out for me and taught me about life," she recalls.

Without a doubt, Joy's chemistry teacher was a prominent female figure who sparked her love for education and influenced her career choices.

When she passed, Joy was devastated. "I cried for weeks. To honor her, I became a teacher myself, and I wanted to become the best chemist I could be."

Joy as a little girl

With this intention, Joy finished high school and went on to study at
the University of West Indies. She graduated with first-class honors in
chemistry. To advance her knowledge, she continued her education in
the United Kingdom, where she got her master's degree in analytical
chemistry. Her thesis received the highest score ever attained at that
university, making her the perfect PhD candidate.

> **"My mother said I brought joy to her heart the moment she
> saw me, which is where my name came from."**

"The faculty offered me a scholarship, but I was so homesick, I had to
decline. I needed to go home," she recalls.

Upon returning to Jamaica, she got a job at Tia Maria, a famous coffee
liquor company, hopeful that it would give her exciting job experience.
Unfortunately, she found her new routine underwhelming.

"I would often look out the window and see a neighboring rum distillery
on the other side of the fence. The people there seemed happy, busy,
and active, so I thought to myself: maybe I should work there?" she
laughs. That distillery was Appleton Estate.

Joy on her first day at the University of the West Indies.

Joy followed her instincts and dropped off her resume next door. Not long after, she got a call, inviting her in for an interview.

"They told me they didn't have any job openings at the time, but the company was so impressed with my CV, they wanted to have a chat anyway," she recalls. "A few weeks later, they offered me a chief chemist position, which they created especially for me."

Although the salary was lower than what she was making at Tia Maria, she accepted the offer. "My friends thought I was crazy, but I saw potential in that job. I didn't see my future making coffee liqueur."

As chief chemist, one of Joy's first tasks was reorganizing the lab and improving its efficiency. During her work, she observed Appleton's previous master blender, Owen Tulloch, spending a lot of time in his private room where he developed new blends.

"I was told nobody was ever allowed to go in there. It was a forbidden zone, and anyone attempting to enter would have to be either very brave or very stupid," she laughs. But Joy's natural curiosity wouldn't let it go. "One day, I came up to him and—with my heart thumping—asked if I could join him and see what he was doing. To my surprise, he said: Sure! No one has ever asked me that before!"

Little did she know, her entire world was about to change.

During her time with Owen, Joy learned about sensory analysis, rum differentiation, the aging process, and blending. He quickly noticed Joy's excellent sensory skills and admired her knowledge of chemistry.

"He told me I had the perfect combination of art and science," she says. "He took me under his wings and taught me everything there is to know about rum. I can say he was my greatest mentor."

Of course, becoming a master blender is not an overnight process. It takes years, sometimes even decades, to thoroughly learn the craft of making rum. Joy worked with Owen for seventeen years until he retired and passed the torch. She took over in 1997, officially making her the first female master blender in the Caribbean and—to our knowledge—the world.

Joy receives an Honorary Doctorate from the University of the West Indies.

"This was a true recognition for my hard work. I was not a family member inheriting the business; I was just a regular employee who had a passion for what I do," she explains. "I can say I earned this position, and I'm happy to be here today, spreading the joy of rum."

Appointing a female master blender caused quite a stir in the spirits industry. But to fully understand the significance of Joy's achievement, one must go back a few decades, when it was unheard of for a woman to go to a bar and enjoy an alcoholic beverage. "When I was growing up in Jamaica, no woman would ever be seen with a drink in her hand, let alone rum. It was not considered elegant or womanly. It was a man's drink. I didn't drink much rum either before I joined Appleton," she tells us.

Since then, Joy has helped transform rum into a sophisticated product that anyone can enjoy. Unfortunately, she still has to deal with some prejudice and disbelief that a woman can make alcohol.

"When I fly for business, custom officers usually ask me what I do. When I answer truthfully, they don't believe me or even test my knowledge, asking me to explain basic things like what rum is," she laughs. "If I said I was a marketing manager, they would probably accept it and ask no questions. Why would I lie that I'm a master blender if it causes me so much trouble?"

"I can say I earned this position, and I'm happy to be here today, spreading the joy of rum."

Joy also recalls when men would turn to her male colleague to discuss business, assuming she was someone's wife. "Sometimes they would continue talking to my colleague instead of me, knowing that I was the one in charge."

Joy's first official picture at Appleton Estate.

Still, Joy doesn't want to focus on the negative. Instead, she tries to bring more positivity to the world. In her spare time, she keeps herself busy with charitable activities, such as her female mentoring program. "I use the wonderful opportunities I've been given to help other women so that they can realize their full potential," she says.

She still teaches chemistry and actively promotes education, arranging scholarships for aspiring students or providing schools with laptops. "As an adopted child, I feel very blessed about all the love and support I experienced growing up. It helped me become successful in my career. I want others to have that opportunity as well."

When asked about the necessary skills of a future master blender, she agrees that a background in chemistry or biochemistry is essential. One must also have excellent sensory skills, a good understanding of the process, and, surprisingly, communication skills.

"In the old days, a master blender was usually tucked away in their secret blending room, but things have changed. These days, a master blender also acts as an ambassador for the brand. They have to travel to conferences, give interviews, and be the face behind the label," she explains.

Joy feels it's a positive development as it empowers consumers: "People want to talk to the expert, not the marketeer. They want to know how their rum was made and who made it. Thanks to modern technology and social media, customers can go to the source and connect with the producer directly, which is what makes this job so diverse."

At the same time, she's excited about the networking opportunities that only strengthened during the pandemic. "I speak at virtual events or conferences almost every week these days. This wasn't so easy in the past as I couldn't travel everywhere," she says. "There are also many new online forums for women in the industry. We're becoming more visible, and it's so much easier to reach out to other women for support, even if they're a few time zones away."

So, will there be more female master blenders in the future? Joy's optimism is infectious.

"To all the women out there who want to work with rum, I'd say don't get overburdened with negative experiences and learn from them. Disappointment is just an opportunity for improvement."

Rum Buck

"I actually developed this straightforward and easy cocktail myself. It's very refreshing and a really lovely combination. For this one, you don't really need these fancy shakers, so everyone can try to make it. Using a solid glass also works. Using a bit more of this or a little bit less of that makes it your own drink."

—Joy

Glass: Highball
Garnish: Lime wedge and straw

2 oz. Appleton Estate 8 yrs.
1 slice of orange
3 drops of aromatic bitters
Splash of Ginger ale

Muddle orange and bitters in a strong glass. Add rum and ice, stir, top with more ice, and then with ginger ale.

Kayla's Tip:
Bitters are the spices of cocktails, where Angostura is "the salt" that fits in just about everything and Peychaud's is "the pepper." When selecting, feel free to experiment.

Good to Know:
This recipe is similar to a classic "Buck" style of drink, the Moscow Mule.

Chapter 3

Ana Lorena Vásquez Ampié, Zacapa, Guatemala

Ana Lorena Vásquez Ampié, or Lorena to friends, is the eldest of six siblings. Growing up on a farm in Nicaragua, she was a bright little girl and a natural supertaster, which meant her parents had difficulty feeding her.

"I refused to drink milk during spring. It always smelled foul to me," Lorena tells us as she tries to recall when she first noticed her extraordinary olfactory talents. "One day, I discovered the reason why it tasted so awful: it was the grass that our cows ate. I could still smell it in the milk."

Her sense of smell was so developed that there was not much she could eat. "My parents were worried because I was very skinny at some point," she laughs. She also squirms as she tells us about her hate for hamburgers and the unappealing texture of the meat. "That's why I learned to cook at an early age. If I didn't like what my parents made for dinner, I prepared something else for myself. This way, I could ensure there was nothing wrong with any ingredients of my food."

At her baptism, a young Lorena poses with her mother.

Today, Lorena is an exceptional cook, and anyone lucky enough to taste one of her culinary creations can attest to her talents.

With such a sensitive nose, Lorena's future had to be connected to rum. However, her career took a different trajectory. Lorena's father was a doctor and owned a local pharmacy, so she was expected to follow in his footsteps. She was a gifted girl with an empirical brain, so she happily chose to study chemistry at a university. Here, she decided to specialize in food technology and embrace student life in a big city.

"To be honest, studying was not my favorite thing to do. I wanted to enjoy myself," she laughs. We're told that Lorena is still the life and soul of the party, lighting up every room she enters with her laughter and vibrant energy.

Unfortunately, in 1978, a civil war broke out in Nicaragua, making partying or studying impossible.

"Sometimes the military would enter the university grounds, and students would be stuck there for days," Lorena recalls as her eyes tear up.

Eventually, the situation forced her to flee to Costa Rica with her infant child, with nothing but milk and a few necessities in her suitcase. From there, she made her way to Guatemala, her then-husband's homeland, determined to build a new future for herself and her family.

> The Nicaraguan Revolution took place between 1978 and 1990. The initial overthrow of the Somoza regime in 1978–79 was a violent event, and the Contra War of the 1980s took the lives of tens of thousands of Nicaraguans.

As a young chemist who needed professional experience, Lorena joined a local brewery as a quality control specialist. She laughs that she never liked Guatemalan beer, but the job matched her qualifications, so she made the best of the opportunity and developed her skill set. Not long after, a rum distillery nearby needed a skilled technician to work in their quality control department, and Lorena was the perfect candidate. She began working for Zacapa in 1984 and fell in love with rum almost immediately. "I entered the premises and got mesmerized by the aroma lingering in the air. It was much better than beer for sure," she laughs.

As soon as she started her job at Zacapa, she developed a strong interest in the aging process and slowly transitioned toward blending responsibilities.

"Distillation and fermentation are technical, but aging is where the magic happens. You can get creative and add your personal touch."

During her transition, she learned all about rum production from her older mentors, who worked in the company for years. However, none of them could match Lorena's impressive skills: a technical background and an ultra-sensitive nose.

"Because I understand chemistry, I can smell the rum and tell whether there was a problem during fermentation," she says.

Still, despite her extraordinary talents, she had to work hard to prove her expertise. "These men worked there for several decades and had always made rum the same way, and here I was, a young woman with a chemistry degree, telling them to change their ways," she laughs. "They resisted at first—until they could taste the difference."

Lorena also experienced difficulties when trying to improve existing systems. She often depended on the information given by her coworkers, who sometimes would omit significant details on purpose.

"They simply didn't trust me," she reflects. "I had to do a lot of my own research and experiment with my own blends because they didn't want to cooperate."

A photograph taken by Lorena's son in 2000 alongside the first bottle of Ron Zacapa X.O.

Despite these challenges, Lorena found a way to win her colleagues' trust: "I took the time to explain everything and showed them that I wasn't trying to undermine their knowledge. I was open to feedback and communication. Eventually, they agreed to try things my way."

Thanks to this relentless determination and a personal quest for perfection, Lorena eventually made her way to the top, introducing numerous innovations to Zacapa.

For one, she has perfected their aging process (known as Solera), making it unique to the brand, and has implemented local traditions for smoking and charring barrels. She also moved Zacapa's aging facilities to the highlands of Guatemala.

The Solera system (*sistema solera*) is a complex technique used for aging and blending rum, which originates from Spain and is now used by Guatemalan rum producers. Lorena has introduced significant improvements to the system, blending younger and older liquids in several types of barrels. For instance, Zacapa 23 is a blend that contains rum aged six to twenty-three years. Lorena also personally selects the cask types and arranges them to create the best liquid.

The thin air and colder climate in high altitudes make the aging process slower, which results in more complex flavors. Zacapa's warehouses are located 7,500 feet (2,300 meters) above sea level, which earned them the poetic name House Above the Clouds.

Introducing these innovations wasn't easy. Lorena often felt like she was riding against the tide, but she was determined to bring her ideas to life. Some of her bosses had a military background and narrow views on how rum should be made.

"Distillation and fermentation are technical, but aging is where the magic happens."

"Sometimes it's better to get forgiveness than permission," she concludes with a famous quote by a female computer pioneer, Grace

Hopper. This old-fashioned way of thinking, perpetuated by many male executives, continues to be one of the many barriers women face in any industry. Still, because of her fearlessness, Lorena earned the freedom to try things her way, transforming Zacapa into the award-winning product it is today.

Following Lorena's story, we notice it's hard to identify one precise moment when she was officially appointed master blender. In her case, it was a natural transition as she grew within the company since joining in 1984.

Lorena smells a freshly toasted barrel.

Back when Lorena joined the company, a woman working at the distillery was a rare sighting. "You'd be more likely to find one at the office than behind the stills," she reflects.

Today, Zacapa is proud to hire more and more women, even in technical or manual roles that are typically male-dominated. It is common to pass by and see a female truck driver or cooper working at the distillery.

With both men and women being able to make high-quality products, why are there still so few female master blenders in the industry? Lorena believes that—among other challenges such as the lack of access to education or societal prejudice—most women struggle with self-imposed limitations.

"If you have the technical knowledge, passion, and excellent sensory skills, then you're fully capable of doing this job," she explains. "But you have to believe in yourself and not be afraid to grab the opportunity, even if you don't see many women working in your niche. There weren't any women blenders when I started, but that didn't stop me because I had the passion for it."

Lorena's passion, however, isn't just limited to the factory. She was the leading force behind the bottle's signature *petate* weave, bringing income opportunities to the women in a local weaver community. Since then, these women have become an integral part of Zacapa's branding.

Zacapa bottles prominently feature a *petate* weave—a traditional Guatemalan decoration typically made of dried palm leaves or grass. In 1999, Zacapa took the initiative to support women from El Quiché who were displaced by conflict, employing them for their *petate* weaving skills. Currently, over seven hundred women are weaving Zacapa's *petate* bands, giving the bottles their Guatemalan authenticity.

Now, Lorena is training two new master blenders, and a woman is amongst them. "I can tell who created the rum just by tasting it. Women pay more attention to the aromas and flavors, resulting in a more nuanced product," she says.

Zacapa Espresso

"I love this one because I am super passionate about coffee. Of course, we have some amazing coffee here in Guatemala. I use this as an espresso shot but without the heat."

—Lorena

Glass: Rocks or espresso
Garnish: Orange peel

1 ¾ oz. Zacapa 23
1 oz. espresso
1 bar spoon Demerara syrup

Shake with ice, double strain into a glass.

Kayla's Tip:
Let your espresso cool before using. To get a beautiful head of foam, utilize a "reverse dry shake" method. Shake with ice, strain into mixing glass with a Hawthorne strainer, shake in a clean shaker, and strain again with a fine mesh strainer.

Good to Know:
Twist an orange peel, a.k.a. orange zest, onto your cocktail to release the oils. When peeling your orange, avoid the pith.

DIY Tip:
To make demerara syrup, simply combine equal parts demerara sugar with water and heat until the sugar completely dissolves. Let cool before using.

Chapter 4

Carmen López de Bastidas, Destilería Carúpano, Venezuela

Carmen López de Bastidas was born and raised in the Venezuelan coastal town of Carúpano, which gave name to the area's renowned rum and the country's national heritage. At an early age, Carmen learned two things: she had a sensitive nose, and she loved her hometown. To her, working as a master blender of Carúpano is a dream come true. Still, she never thought she could make a career out of her sensory talents, let alone in her hometown.

Like many young Venezuelans, Carmen moved to Caracas to study at the university. She obtained a chemistry degree and got her first job as a quality control specialist. Her big city life didn't last long as Carmen had to return home for family reasons, though she now calls it destiny. "It was meant to be. I had to be at the right place, at the right time," she recalls.

Carmen as a teenager

As soon as she got back, the local rum manufacturer of Destilería Carúpano reached out to her, offering to lead their newly-created quality control department. She was reluctant at first because she knew nothing about rum and consumed little of it, but the company assured her they would train her and teach her everything there was to know about the distillate. She accepted the job with mixed feelings and officially joined Destilería Carúpano in January 1990. "Thank God I said yes because I totally fell in love with my career," she laughs.

Carúpano has been a family-owned business since 1762, with ambitious hopes to expand to the international market. For this reason, the company needed to standardize its production system to ensure consistency and quality. To do so, they needed someone with a strong chemistry background, and they entrusted Carmen with this colossal task.

Hacienda Altamira (the estate where Carúpano is based) was
founded in 1762, meaning its legacy spans over 260 years. A master
blender typically overlooks the aging process and the quality of
the distillates. At the end of the last century, Carúpano decided to
outsource the production of sugar cane alcohol from a third party,
but Carmen still has to ensure that the quality of the rum matches
the company requirements.

"They told me I was the heart and brain of the plant and that I should
do whatever I thought was necessary to help the company grow," she
recalls. Eventually, she was officially promoted to master blender, the
first woman in Venezuela to hold this title.

As part of her training, Carmen had to try all kinds of flavors and create
a significant memory of tastes in her mind. "There's a lot of technical
knowledge involved, but you also have to trust your instincts and palate,"
she explains.

Carmen in the Ron Carúpano warehouse.

While her bosses and coworkers noticed her golden nose nearly straight
away, she remains humble. "Practice makes perfect," she says, "and I was
lucky to have great teachers."

Her most notable mentor included Dr. Giancarlo Mazzocchi, who had just retired from another prominent Venezuelan brand. "He would teach me in six two-hour sessions, spread over six months. After that, I was on my own," she recalls. "He taught me valuable lessons like how to blend, use all the instruments, and measure an alcoholic degree. Still, I had to start from scratch and create Carúpano's quality standards on my own."

Dr. Mazzocchi also taught her how to reduce tannic acid levels in a spirit and make it smoother. "Men often like the hard, tannic notes, but I always felt there was too much of it in the rum," Carmen explains. "I want my product to be mystical, magical, and balanced. By lowering the tannic notes, rum becomes more feminine and seductive," she elaborates with a spark in her eye.

In spirits production, lowering the tannic acid is typically achieved by charring or toasting the barrels. The charred wood acts as a filter, changing or eliminating various congeners in the distillate.

So far, Carmen's career sounds as smooth as her rum, but behind the scenes, things weren't always easy. "Suddenly, I became the boss of a team that consisted entirely of men much older and experienced than me," she says. "I was there to standardize our processes and formulas. I had to give them instructions and change their routines. Of course, there was some resistance."

One of Carmen's toughest challenges was convincing her coworkers that their way of doing things was flawed. "Naturally, they rejected my ideas because they thought their approach worked well for so many years. Why fix something that's not broken?" she explains. Indeed, changes are never easy, but this was a particularly tough nut to crack.

Carmen savors Ron Carúpano's aromas

"Imagine rum as a kind of soup. These men have been making this soup for decades, recreating it from memory and experience. If the soup didn't taste good, they just added an extra ingredient to make it taste better. Now imagine a small woman appearing out of nowhere, telling them that there are quality guidelines they need to follow," she laughs.

Carmen proceeds to say that not only was she the first person to create rum formulas and standardize the production process in Carúpano, but she was also the first woman with so much authority.

Carmen's formulation standard also applies to producers in third-party companies. To control sugarcane alcohol quality, Carúpano assigns a restriction or minimal to elements in the spirit. The alcohol can only be certified and admitted when the standards are met for each element.

"I had to work hard to prove my expertise and used a lot of technical words that had never been used before. But my coworkers believed there was nothing wrong with their product. Why should they listen to me, a young woman with less experience? It's always a challenge when a lady enters a man's playground and starts to move things around," she reflects. She often felt underestimated or even ignored by her male colleagues, making her efforts difficult.

Despite the initial obstacles, Carmen thinks they were a natural reaction to change and holds no grudges. "Yes, there were some bumps on the road, but now I'm fully accepted, and all the men on our team are super proud of the delicious soup they make now," she laughs. Indeed, thanks to her, Carúpano is an internationally renowned brand with countless awards and honors in the rum world.

> "I want my product to be mystical, magical, and balanced.
> By lowering the tannic notes, rum becomes more feminine
> and seductive."

To make the most out of her days, she showed up at work at 7:00 a.m. sharp and took care of her family in the afternoon. "The long hours were not imposed by the company. It was my choice, out of solidarity with the workers who were highly committed to our product," she recalls.

Because she was so busy, she didn't think of networking or making herself visible as a woman master blender. This changed during a conference at the Metropolitan University of Granada, where Carmen gave a speech. "Afterward, people would approach me and ask why I was hiding this entire time," she laughs.

Because of this tireless effort to achieve excellence, people finally saw Carmen's contributions to the rum industry and recognized Carúpano as a premium drink.

"I look for beauty in flavors, and I'm happy others can see it, too."

Carmen says that she's incredibly proud of her formulas, which helped Carúpano become an internationally renowned brand. "I look for beauty in flavors, and I'm happy others can see it, too," she tells us. "I also want other women to see that they can achieve anything if they have the passion and put it in the work."

Fortunately, social media is making it easier to network and spread the rum gospel from a distance. "Social networking brings wonderful opportunities and makes it much easier for women to be visible in our industry. It's a positive development, and I'm sure there will be more female rum producers in the future.

So what's next for Carúpano? Since creating rum is a lot of work around the clock, master blenders usually have a trainee or assistant take over their duties on their off days. As we speak, Carmen is coaching a new master blender that will follow in her footsteps.

"The goal is to ensure that the palette of flavors remains consistent and doesn't get reformulated again," she explains.

Carmen smiles at a local tasting.

After evaluating all the candidates based on skills and talent, Carmen is happy to say the company chose another woman. She is also happy to tell all the young women considering a career in the rum industry: "Do not be afraid to trust that you are talented, to trust that you are strong, and to trust in your sensibility. Once you believe that you have these three qualities, welcome to the amazing world of rum!"

Reflecting on the qualities women can bring into the production process, Carmen is confident that Carúpano rum is female.

"Women have a different view on taste than men. It's the mysticism and seductiveness I mentioned earlier. To me, rum should be exquisite, beautiful, and satisfying to the palate. Carúpano wants to keep these qualities, which is why they are happy to have found another future female master blender."

As Carmen elaborates on what Venezuelan rum means to her, she pauses as her eyes tear up.

"When you have a bottle of Carúpano in your home, you have a bit of Venezuela. It's our heritage, and we respect our rum tradition deeply. I want all people to know that Venezuela is a wonderful country, and Carúpano rum represents that."

Carmen's Cocktail

"This one is made in my honor and directly assembled in the glass since it works on densities. It is mainly made from the wrist since each layer is as high as the other ones. Because of the condensed milk, this is an excellent digestive or dessert cocktail."

—Carmen

This cocktail is made by **Carlos Bustamante** of Alto Restaurant.

Glass: Martini
Garnish: Cinnamon stick

70 percent pure chocolate liqueur (all equal layers—see tips below)
Condensed milk
Coffee liqueur
Ron Carúpano 21

This needs to be "layered." Fill the glass in order of reading, so the rum ends on top.

Kayla's Tip:
To keep a layered cocktail cold, chill your ingredients. To layer, slowly pour down the side of the glass or over the back of a bar spoon.

Good to Know:
Layering is only possible when the density of each liquid is higher than that above. Your most dense ingredient must go on the bottom and your least dense (your rum) will float on top.

Chapter 5

Stéphanie Dufour, Dillon & Depaz, Martinique

Stéphanie Dufour is the cellar master of Dillon & Depaz in the verdant island of Martinique. And much like the rum that comes from the island, she embodies its nuances and the full spectrum of taste (not just its sweetness). Though we can assure you, Stéphanie is the sweetest person you'll ever meet.

To fully understand the passion that drives her work, we need to go back in time. Stéphanie grew up on a cattle farm in Dordogne, southern France. She had a great appreciation and respect for the organic world and would often ride horses through the forest, inhaling the lush scents of nature. That's when she first realized she had an extraordinary sense of smell.

"I remember smelling something particular one day. When I investigated, it turned out it was the truffles in the ground. Usually, only dogs or pigs can discover them. My family often joked that my nose is just as effective, but I'm much better company," she laughs.

Soon, Stéphanie decided to cultivate her passion for plants, studying agronomy and later specializing in viticulture and enology. "I was interested in different transformation processes and achieving a quintessence of flavors through agricultural ingredients," she explains.

As a young graduate, she joined Courvoisier, a large cognac brand from the Charente region of France, to examine elements that contribute to the perception of smoothness or freshness in a spirit. To understand how a spirit would develop in the future, Stéphanie also studied the effects of wood, pressure, and humidity.

After Courvoisier, she created 150 alcoholic and nonalcoholic beverage processes and assembly studies for a liqueur company—in less than ten months.

"I learned so much in that short period. It allowed me to go deeper into the techniques of transformation found in grinding, cooking, fermentation, distillation, and evaporation. I also learned about a fundamental rule: the order of inserting the ingredients. For instance, mixing A with B and then with C would result in a different product than combining C with B and then A. It's super fascinating," she tells us with a sparkle in her eye.

> Typically, when two ingredients mix or react, adding a third won't have a huge effect on the end result. This is the rule of saturation. For instance, if you put a tea bag in water and then add sugar, you will taste the herbal notes more than if you put a teabag in already sweetened water. The sugar prevents the tea from releasing its full flavor due to the water saturation (the point at which the liquid can't dissolve any more ingredients).

After working with cognac and liqueur, Stéphanie moved on to a premium grape vodka known as Cîroc. "I had never made such a product before, so I was surprised by how easily I could create it without any real doubt. All I did was follow my nose and trust my knowledge of plant behavior."

Her instincts were so remarkable that she could figure out the composition of a liquid without tasting it. "One of my colleagues asked me to work out the ingredients in a product just by smelling it. I can still picture the astonishment on his face when I named each element correctly. I had a tough time back then as I was the only woman on the team," she reflects with a bit of sadness behind her smile.

Although she didn't have any female mentors, she remembers a few people fondly. Her tequila teacher, Carlos Camarena, master distiller at La Alteña Distillery, taught her to think of herself as an artist who composes beautiful flavors.

Stéphanie visits a tequila producer.

In just a few years, Stéphanie learned to produce almost every type of alcohol: cognac, liqueur, gin, vodka, whisky, wine, beer, and tequila. *Rhum*, however, remained her favorite, most likely because its production is the closest to cognac, one of the national spirits of France.

"Both spirits are seasonal, which can be short and quite stressful due to time constraints. It inspired me to develop a process that produces a fresh spirit faster, reduces overall costs, and retains the original taste."

Her adventure with rum didn't begin until she met Robert Leaute, who invited her to work on his new rum project in Guadeloupe. "He said he needed a feminine eye. We made the first batch of rum in Guadeloupe, and then it quickly evolved into a French West Indies blended rum. It allowed me to learn all about *rhum agricole*, which sparked my curiosity about the nature of sugarcane.

> *Rhum agricole* is the French-protected term for sugarcane juice rum, a style of rum originally distilled in the French Caribbean islands only from freshly squeezed sugarcane juice.

Although she remains extremely humble about her achievements, it is clear her work has a massive impact on anyone who tastes her creations. She visibly lights up when she tells us about her greatest reward: to see someone's face change as her rum evokes different sensations.

Stéphanie extracts rhum from a barrel for sampling.

"I want to keep the sensation of nature in my rum. When you find a beautiful flavor, you want to keep it. I'm happy others can appreciate it, too."

Stéphanie oversees the rum barrel aging process in the Depaz cellars.

For the sake of flavor, Stéphanie hopes there will be more women in the world of rum. "Being the only woman feels lonely sometimes, and it requires me to change my character and be more 'male.' I'd love to have more room for my femininity. Rum producers can benefit from both traits. Men go for impact, and women focus on the longevity of flavor," she reflects.

"I want to keep the sensation of nature in my rum. When you find a beautiful flavor, you want to keep it. I'm happy others can appreciate it, too."

As more women consider a career in rum, Stéphanie reminds them to channel instinctual passions.

"It's like when I used to jump with my horses. When it needs to be done, we jump. We can't hesitate or discuss; we must jump," she says. "Men grab an opportunity without questioning whether they are good enough or qualified enough. They get out of their comfort zone and go for it. We should be like that, too."

Islands Swimming Pool

"This cocktail is really me. When I drink this somewhere outside Martinique, I am back on the island for the duration of the cocktail. A culture caught in a drink."

—Stéphanie

Glass: Champagne coupe or flute
Garnish: A flower

1 oz. Depaz White
1 teaspoon/bar spoon Dormoy white hibiscus syrup
Splash of champagne

Fill mixing glass with ice, stir rum and syrup, and strain into a flute or coupe glass. Top with champagne.

Kayla's Tip:
I recommend a dry sparkling white wine. Make sure your flower garnish is edible or opt for lemon zest.

DIY Tip:
To make hibiscus syrup:
- Boil water and let cool.
- Add 5g white hibiscus tea (or 10g fresh white hibiscus flowers) to 100g of hot water.
- Let steep and strain through a fine-mesh sieve.
- Warm 100g of castor sugar and half the hibiscus "tea" in a pot until sugar dissolves. Do not boil.
- Remove from heat and let cool.

Chapter 6

Miriam Paola Pacheco, Casa Tarasco Spirits, Mexico

Surrounded by a series of small bottles filled with a gorgeous golden liquid, Mexican master blender Miriam Paola Pacheco keeps herself busy at Casa Tarasco. Today, her hectic schedule includes a quality check of various charanda samples. "You're welcome to come and help me out," she laughs as she tells us how much she enjoys comparing different flavors and colors.

Casa Tarasco is currently one of the few charanda distilleries left in Michoacán, a state that used to boast almost one hundred liquor manufacturers.

Michoacán is a state in western Mexico known for its prominent fishing industry. The area is also abundant in avocados and berries, with more than 30,000 avocado orchards producing about 80 percent of Mexico's total avocado crop. The state also grows almost all of Mexico's blackberries and strawberries.

Not many people know of Mexican rum, let alone charanda, which is native to the Uruapan area. The spirit was granted a Protected Designation of Origin in 2003 and has a distinct flavor due to higher sugar, sucrose, and iron levels. Like rum, charanda is derived from sugarcane. Named after a hill where the first distillery was built, *charanda* means red-colored soil in the locally spoken Purépecha language (also called Tarascan). The volcanic soil is what gives the local sugarcane and the charanda its unique taste.

Asked about the name, Miriam explains that the noun used to be of the feminine gender in Spanish, *la charanda*. However, the authorities changed the article to the masculine *el charanda*. "Even the word is not welcome to be a woman," she jokes, "let alone the person who makes the rum."

The locals continue to refer to the spirit with its original feminine form, and Miriam can say that *la charanda* runs in her genes.

> Like charanda, the noun tequila also comes with masculine and feminine forms (*el* and *la* tequila), though most native speakers prefer using the masculine article nowadays.

Before Miriam ran the company alongside her brother, Fernando, the Pacheco family had a long tradition of making mezcal. But the business wasn't going as well as expected, so in 1907, Miriam's great-grandfather, José Cleofas, decided to distill sugarcane.

Miriam's great-grandfather, Don José, (right) and a worker (left) at Casa Tarasco.

Mezcal is a type of distilled alcoholic beverage made from cooked and fermented parts of agave plants.

Casa Tarasco uses sugarcane to make a low-proof molasses-based charanda for the locals (35 percent alcohol), containing only 20 percent of pure sugarcane juice. For higher markets, they produce a spirit of 40–46 percent alcohol, using only fresh juice. The local charanda variety is cheaper due to the lower alcohol content. Still, it's a popular beverage for many young Mexicans who like to drink it with coke or soda.

In the early days, the standard rum production technique involved hard sugarcane caramel for enhanced flavor, which the distiller would often dissolve in warm water. This method proved to be more sustainable for the family as mezcal production is typically limited to harvest season. Not to mention that sugarcane is much easier to grow than agave. Eventually, charanda became Casa Tarasco's primary produce and a cornerstone of its success.

Miriam's great-grandmother (left) alongside Miriam's grandmother (right)

Unfortunately, Don José soon became unwell. That's where Miriam's biggest inspiration came in: her great-grandmother, Cleo. She took over the distillery in the early 1940s and helped grow the company. Most notably, she introduced the handmade autograph on the label, which became a vital element of Casa Tarasco's branding.

> **"Even the word [*la charanda*] is not welcome to be a woman, let alone the person who makes the rum."**

Of course, a woman leading a distillery was unheard of in those days. "People thought my great-grandmother should just stay home with her husband and take care of her ten children," Miriam explains.

And yet, Cleo persevered and helped make Casa Tarasco's charanda the quality product it is today. "Growing up as a little girl, I always wanted to be like her," Miriam tells us. Even though Cleo never officially held the title of a master blender, for all we know, she was the first woman in Mexico to produce this spirit.

Miriam with her father

As Miriam tells us about her childhood, her eyes brighten up with happiness. "Everyone knew our home as *La Bohemia*. Families came to the distillery to celebrate Las Posadas, enjoying the holidays with piñatas and smelling delicious charanda in the air."

As a little girl, Miriam had a keen interest in how things worked in the company, offering to help with various tasks, such as sticking labels on bottles. "People would come by with empty jugs every day to fill them with charanda fresh from the barrels," she recalls. "We also sold bottles on the street, just a few meters away from our house."

> Las Posadas is a religious festival celebrated in Mexico and some parts of the United States between December 16 and 24.

Miriam and her brother Fernando still live on the distillery grounds. Even though she always knew she wanted to continue the family tradition, Miriam still went to university to pursue a degree. "The subject of my studies didn't matter to me. My life and my dream job were here at Casa Tarasco."

Miriam's passion for her community goes beyond Casa Tarasco. In an effort to distract the neighborhood children from crime, she runs a local music school with her family. She firmly believes that singing and playing instruments can make them more sensitive and open to different cultures. "Music keeps children away from trouble and gives them a better future," she explains. "Creativity expands their horizons."

> Miriam's hometown is no longer the idyllic place it used to be. As the production of avocado is the main source of income for many farmers, local "avocado gangs" terrorize the people of Michoacán in search of "green gold." To gain control over the sector, extortion and threats of public hangings and dismemberments are common practices.

Still, Miriam's had to face many obstacles in her career. "Many people think spirits are manly and should therefore be made for men and produced by men. There is little room for women in this space," she clarifies.

This reality becomes clear whenever she visits a bar in Mexico to sell Casa Tarasco products. "Men prefer to talk to my male colleague. I was also told that our labels should read *el charanda* instead of *la charanda* because a feminine article indicates poor quality."

"The subject of my studies didn't matter to me. My life and my dream job were here at Casa Tarasco."

Miriam remains optimistic that the landscape is changing and women are more accepted in the spirits industry. But there's still a long way to go. "We need to believe in ourselves more and realize that we can do anything. Only then will we be able to convince others that we are truly capable."

Miriam "works" the land at Casa Tarasco.

Germain Tarasco

"I like many cocktails, and like in a restaurant, I want to try different things from the chef. I simply want to find other flavors, and therefore I want to find old recipes about how they used to drink in the old days."

—Miriam

Glass: Goblet
Garnish: Berries, rosemary, and lavender

1½ oz. Charanda Blanca
1 oz. seasonal berry shrub
1 oz. St. Germain
¼ oz. lemon juice

Add all ingredients to mixing glass, shake with ice, and double strain into a goblet.

> **Kayla's Tip:**
> The original version called for a "berry vinaigrette," but as each vinaigrette will have a unique level of sour/sweet, here's a simple recipe for a homemade shrub that works beautifully in this drink. It's highly customizable, so tailor it to your favorite flavors.
>
> All measurements are by mass:
> - Add 1 part demerara sugar and 1 part water to a pot
> - Bring to a boil on the stove; stir occasionally
> - Reduce to a simmer and add in ½ part seasonal berries
> - Simmer for ten minutes on the lowest heat possible
> - Add ½ part apple cider vinegar
> - Stir and remove from heat
> - Strain through a fine-mesh sieve and let cool before using.
>
> **Bonus Tip:** The strained berries make a fantastic jam!

Chapter 7

Carol Homer-Caesar, Angostura Limited, Trinidad & Tobago

Few rum distilleries can claim a high number of female employees, much less many female rum manufacturers who have never felt out of place because of their gender. Carol Homer-Caesar, master blender of Angostura Limited, insists women blended rum long before the company officially created that title, so she is confident that the rum revolution is already underway.

"All the women I know in the rum industry, especially in blending, bring balance, romance, innovation, and certainly passion to rum making," she says.

Carol was born in the southern part of Trinidad, San Fernando, an area rich in farmlands, sugarcane, and a keen community interested in the energy sector. She is the middle child of the family, having grown up with three sisters and three brothers. Her father worked in a laboratory at a local oil company and often brought little Carol to work, memories that would influence her later interest in the sciences.

Carol secured her first job at the Caribbean Industrial Research Institute. Here, she developed her skills as an analytical chemist, working with a wide range of products like food, beverages, water, and pharmaceuticals. "I was responsible for developing test methods and laboratory techniques, using analytical instrumentation, and training the laboratory staff," she recalls.

A young Carol at the St. Gabriel's Girls R.C. School

At the institute, she also achieved a notable International Laboratory Accreditation—ISO 17025, the main standard used by testing and calibration laboratories. Then, after fifteen years, she discovered an exciting opportunity to manage Angostura Limited. In 1995, she became head of the laboratory. As she worked with aged rums, it became clear that she found her true calling.

"All the women I know in the rum industry, especially in blending, bring balance, romance, innovation, and certainly passion to rum making."

"It was an eye-opener," she recalls. "I was evaluating products to make the connection between the chemical components which gave the best aroma and flavor in aged liquids. That's where I really started to develop and became very interested in actually creating blends one day."

Angostura Limited started in 1824 and is most famous for its bitters, which remain its most well-known product and flagship brand. The company began to blend its first rum in the early 1900s, but that side of the business only took off in 1949 when Angostura built an ultra-modern distillery—Trinidad Distillers Limited—with its five-column still.

Before joining Angostura Limited, Carol had never worked with rum and was anxious to learn all about its production. "The oak barrels stacked up on pallets high up to the ceiling made me curious, and that smell was unforgettable," she swoons.

She soon started to experiment with the aging process and observed the impact of various alcohol percentages or the location of the aging liquid. She also adjusted the process to different temperatures and humidity, so every little detail was noted.

"I also tried changing the type of casks and experimented with sherry and cognac barrels," she explains. "As my knowledge developed, in 1999, I started to create my first blends, but on a laboratory level. After sensory evaluations of these blends, my executives were confident that I was ready for something bigger."

With her expert chemistry background, it was clear she was the perfect person to bring Angostura Rum to the next level.

"All we had until that point was the standard white, gold, and dark rum. We didn't have premium rums in the markets. That only happened with the introduction of the Angostura 1919, followed by Angostura 1824 and the rest of the premium rum range."

As cocktails grew in popularity, consumers demanded more flavors, so many rum producers used to offer three basic varieties: white, gold, and dark. White rum was typically used to give cocktails a sharper edge, while dark rum was more mellow or sweeter. The color often had nothing to do with aging but with the adding of caramel.

As Angostura continued to hire more women, its rum production continued to increase significantly, showing that the global appreciation for this noble spirit is growing. "It's a fantastic development. Some consumers don't just want premium aged rums nowadays but also flavored and spiced rums. There's a lot of room for innovation," Carol reflects.

As she tells us, she became able to recognize the components of the rum through smell alone, and she could also identify those aged rums that would create the best balance in a premium blend. This type of work requires uninterrupted concentration, so Carol always starts her day at 6:00 a.m. when the manufacturing plants are quiet.

"I love coming to the laboratory early in the morning when there's nobody around, and I have space to release my creative energy! This is when I can really interact with the rums and feel free to create my rum blends."

Carol samples different rums in the Angostura tasting room

Carol tells us she created the Angostura Legacy blend this way, which remains one of her proudest achievements. "I wasn't told anything apart from, 'Go and make the most expensive rum in the world.' There was no product brief, no benchmark from the marketing department instructing me on the taste profile or aroma notes to develop." She adds with a radiant smile: "I started with a clean slate, and it was extremely exciting."

Angostura Legacy was created to celebrate the fiftieth anniversary of Trinidad's independence in 2012, with only twenty decanters ever made. Legacy by Angostura is presented in a bespoke 500ml crystal and silver decanter specially made by jewelers to the Prince of Wales, Asprey of London. Carol used seven of the best-aged rums with different profiles to create this special blend, with the youngest rum being seventeen years old.

Officially, the company did not have a dedicated rum master blender until 2013. But, as Carol explains, Angostura always had a team working on rum blends, so appointing one master blender did not seem appropriate.

"Blending will always be a team effort," she says. "If you're such a big company, no one person can do that. So, of course, when I joined the team in 1995, there was already a group of people doing it." Later, she adds: "In essence, I became the first master blender of the company, and I'm still the only master blender in Trinidad and Tobago."

Although Carol became the first official master blender of Angostura, she wasn't the first woman creating blends for the company. When she joined, Vidia Persad-Doodnath, another chemist, was an executive in the laboratory and blending department until she retired in 2014. In fact, seeing female employees is not a rarity in the company. Angostura prides itself in hiring many women across all levels in the organization, and we're told 61 percent of the management staff is female.

Besides training, Carol is in charge of the entire operations department, which keeps her busy. Right now, her position is Chief Operating Officer (Ag.). This means she's responsible for everything in operations—overlooking the distillery, the wastewater treatment plant, new product development, bottling, warehousing, quality assurance, and shipping. Oh, and yes, also blending!

Currently, Carol is training a new team of future blenders. "The blending team that is operational today consists entirely of women," which means Angostura's new products are entirely female-led. "We have created Angostura No. 1 Limited edition and luxury rum type together," she adds.

Angostura Limited has won over 150 international highly acclaimed awards for its rum throughout the last twelve years, resulting from a well-coordinated, talented, and dedicated blending team of women focused on creating some of the best rums in the world.

With such a high percentage of women working in management at their company, Angostura Limited is a great ambassador for diversity and women in the rum industry.

"It is important to educate people about that. Over the last forty years, more women have entered the spirits world. Most of these women start in quality control, then move into blending and eventually become spirit ambassadors, which is a natural progression. It's not just a man's world anymore."

It's clear she sees the prospects for women in the spirits industry in bright colors, and she's confident that the future of rum is female. When reflecting on the unique qualities female professionals can bring into the industry, she says: "We have a high level of commitment, discipline, dedication, and focus. I see this with all my female staff at both management and non-management levels, involved in all stages, from fermentation, distillation, wastewater treatment until the final aging. I think we can develop an intimate connection with rum."

Carol delivers a speech

To Carol, these qualities, especially consistency and meticulousness, are necessary for the rum industry; you cannot make mistakes or slip up; you must follow the set course of policies and procedures. She continues: "Aging the best rums is almost like raising children, from that raw molasses fermentation stage, all the way to rum maturity. We'll check in on them along the way, making sure they have the best virtues and morals and that at the end of the day, they blossom into something spectacular!"

Mai Tai

"My love for the Mai Tais came as a result of joy for authentic flavors that are well balanced. I would often request my favorite at the 'Rum Cocktails by Angostura' cocktail bar. I would order three Mai Tais, sometimes more, as I am always having friends over."

—Carol

Glass: Highball
Garnish: A fresh mint sprig

1 ½ oz. Angostura 7 yrs.
¾ oz. orange liqueur
1 oz. fresh lime juice
1 oz. Orgeat
2 drops Angostura bitters

Add all ingredients to mixing glass, shake with ice, and double strain over clean ice into highball glass.

Kayla's Tip:
Cointreau, Grand Marnier, and Pierre Lafond are three widely available orange liquors.

DIY Tip:
To make orgeat: Add equal parts sugar, water, and unsalted almonds in a high-speed blender. Blend until smooth and strain through a cheesecloth. For a toasted taste, opt for roasted almonds. For a cleaner taste, try blanched almonds.

Chapter 8

Karen Hoskin, Montanya Distillers, USA

Karen Hoskin, the founder and owner of Montanya Distillers, was the first female keynote speaker at the American Distilling Institute. When she asked her audience of 1,500 to look around and count how many women were in the room, she proved a point: the spirits industry has a problem. Today, she is the driving force behind The Women's Distillery Guild, changing the American craft rum scene as we know it.

Her home in the beautiful Rocky Mountains is a most fitting backdrop— like these mountains, Karen is strong, focused, and aiming to touch the sky. She is a true entrepreneur, sustainability leader, and zero-waste advocate, fearlessly changing the world around her.

Karen was born in New York City, but her family escaped the urban life and moved to rural Maine when she was two years old. She went to college in Massachusetts, where she first noticed her preference for finer spirits.

A young Karen enjoys nature.

"I never drank beer. I was never one of those people who wanted to go to keg parties," she laughs. "I've always been picky about alcohol, so I created a little speakeasy in my dorm. I would invite people over for some Amaretto sours or Kahlua drinks, though it wasn't very sophisticated back in 1986."

In her junior year, Karen took a break and went to India. She stayed with a traditional family to learn Hindi for half a year. "Hindus don't drink, so I didn't have anything for six months," she explains. One day, Karen decided to hop on a train and explore Goa, which was not as culturally restrictive. "I went to a bar in Baga Beach and asked the bartender for a drink that wasn't beer or port," she says. "So he pulled a bottle of Old Monk (an iconic Indian rum) off the shelf. Now I find it too sweet and with too many colorings, but my palate wasn't very evolved at that point. It was the beginning of something epic in my life."

Karen's trip to India started her love affair with rum, but she didn't think of it as a career option until much later. She resumed her college degree, got her master of science in epidemiology (yes, you read that right!), and worked ten years in the public health sector. She never stopped exploring new flavors, though, and developed a strong preference for Central and South American rums.

Karen with her son Nathaniel in India

"Over time, I cultivated a real love for this spirit," she explains. "I like Caribbean rums, too, but they often contain a sulfur element on the palate. The taste profile I enjoy the most is fresh sugarcane juice, so I love *clairin* from Haiti or *rhum agricole* from Martinique."

Clairin is a national alcoholic spirit of Haiti, typically distilled from spontaneously fermented sugarcane juice. It bears a lot of resemblance to rum produced in French overseas areas, called *rhum agricole*.

Karen also grew interested in craft cocktails long before they became a thing. "At the time, you couldn't go to a bar and order a beautiful cocktail infused with homemade ingredients as you can now. So, I started making them myself and served them to my friends at dinner parties," she tells us. This hobby led her to open a rum bar, the only one in the mountains of Colorado, which turned out to be a huge success. "The place was shoulder-to-shoulder packed for every hour that it was open," she smiles.

As she traveled to new rum destinations in her spare time, Karen's passion for rum only kept growing. One day, she visited Guatemala,

where she experienced Ron Zacapa and learned all about the work of
Lorena Vasquez.

"I fell in love with the brand and its story. The whole mountain tradition
of rum was new to me, but it also made me think. I realized this could also
be done in Colorado."

Rum is mainly associated with beach drinks and the Caribbean,
but it also has a rich mountain history. Some of the top rums in the
world are aged at high altitudes. The thin air and colder climate in
the mountains make the aging process slower, which results in more
complex flavors.

Although the idea of making rum in the mountains had already started
brewing in her mind, it didn't fully materialize until much later. It took
another career change at a Fortune 500 company before Karen started
asking herself: what's next?

Then, on a family trip to Belize, Karen learned about a woman named
Marie Sharp, the creator of carrot-based hot sauce. "I started researching
and learning all about her company and how she used this sauce to
change the entire fortunes of her country," she recalls. "It really inspired
me. So, I said to my husband: 'I want to make rum.'"

Today, Montanya is truly making a difference, being a certified B Corp
and recognized as a Best for the World company.

"It was the first time that I had a business of my own that felt deeply
impactful to the environment. I have to be very aware of things like the
supply chain, how things are grown, agricultural products, transportation,
paper, and packaging. It's wonderful because I have a tangible way to
make a difference," Karen adds.

Karen's passion for the environment started in childhood. Her family lived next to a small pond in Winthrop, Maine, and she often debated with her attorney father about their responsibility to protect it. At the time, the EPA was trying to preserve the black duck habitat on her family's newly acquired pond. She and her dad ended up on opposite sides of the argument. Eventually, her father became a board member of the National Audubon Society and a vocal advocate for bird species on waterways in Maine.

As soon as the distillery started running, Karen hired her first employee—a woman named Delena Aseere—and didn't waste any time.

"We would get in the truck and fill it with as many cases of rum as we could fit. We would drive out and not come home until we'd sold every case. That was our deal," she tells us. "We were motivated because I had two small kids, and I couldn't be gone for that long. So, we would just drive around and visit bartenders and liquor stores and sell it right out of the truck."

Outdoors, Karen displays new bottles of Montanya Rum.

Karen's efforts and determination paid off as her rum was met with lots of enthusiasm. "We were one of the first craft distillers in the state," she explains. "Now, there are at least one hundred more, but we were an unknown and strange phenomenon at that point, and people were excited."

Montanya Distillers is a Best for the World honoree due to its environmental, workforce, community, supplier, customer, and corporate governance practices. It ranks in the top 10 percent of all B Corps across all impact areas. Montanya is also the only distillery to earn spots on two Best For lists: Best for the World Overall and Best for the Environment.

Whether it's selling bottles out of a trunk or incorporating sustainability initiatives, it's clear that there's nothing "traditional" about Karen's methods. So, when she had to run a distillery, she learned the technical know-how in the most nontraditional way yet, by shadowing experienced distillers and experts—and asking thousands of questions.

> "It was the first time that I had a business of my own that felt deeply impactful to the environment. It's wonderful because I have a tangible way to make a difference."

One such expert was Jake Norris, then of Stranahan's Colorado Whiskey. "He was one of the first craft distillers here in Colorado, and he is a gem. I would tour around with him and spend time with his stills. He answered so many questions over the years and never doubted that I could pull this off."

Karen also connected with the distillers at Peach Street Distillers and found valuable resources through the American Distillers Institute (ADI). "Back then, ADI was the only place with forums where members could ask questions and get answers from high-level people. That was a big deal for me." The only downside, however, was it was entirely comprised of men.

As a result, Karen is now committed to helping other women in the industry, mentoring three to four different female founders, company owners, or head distillers at a time—in addition to working with both the Female Founders venture group and Women of the Vine and Spirits group.

"It's something I wish I had. I find it inspiring to be in a room of eight hundred women working in the alcohol beverage space, supporting and learning from each other."

She also makes great efforts to keep her company diverse and reflective of American society. "Our company is about 52 percent women, and our leadership team is 60 percent female. It's the balance that creates the best environment. I always try to have Montanya reflect the national reality. We should be at least 20 percent employees of color, and we're achieving it, even in a tiny little mountain ski town that is 98 percent white."

Even outside of her distillery, Karen pushes for more representation. "I have been a correspondent for the *Distiller* magazine for four years. I often write about problematic issues like gender imbalance and lack of sustainability in the rum industry, even though I'm asked not to. Being on these panels with international distillers and talking about these things can be risky and confronting, but I speak my truth."

Still, even though Karen has moved mountains, running a spirits business as a woman doesn't come without slippery slopes. People often mistake her for someone with no decision-making ability, and her choices are questioned more often than those of her male peers.

"I'll never forget walking into a vendor to buy a pump at an event," she recalls. "The salesman talked to me because I was the only person in the booth. But as soon as a man walked in, he stopped talking to me. When I complained, he shut me off, implying that I couldn't possibly be a customer."

Karen visits the Montanya warehouse.

The same goes for gaining the respect of their investors or access to financial resources. "One time, I was making an annual presentation about my company to a group of investors who hadn't met me yet," Karen recalls. "I walked into the room, and they asked me what I brought them for lunch."

Montanya's Distillery & Tasting Room is located at:

212 Elk Avenue
Crested Butte, CO 81224

In recent years, the bar has expanded from 800 to 2,400 square feet, with indoor and outdoor seating.

In Karen's experience, her male peers often raise funds more easily, even though Montanya performs much better than their businesses. "On one occasion, I reached out to the founder of a company similar to mine. I had to understand why I couldn't access capital the way these colleagues of mine were. And he looked me straight in the eye and said, 'It's because you're a woman,' " she says. "That was the moment when I started to realize that women only get 2.8 percent of venture capital in America."[10]

> Believe it or not, gender discrimination is ingrained so deeply into the fabric of our society, even in the twenty-first century; banks only lend 4 percent of their funds to female startups,[11] and in the distilling world, those numbers are even worse.

Still, Karen doesn't get halted by frustration. Instead, she follows her instincts. As Karen reflects on her career with the Rocky Mountains stretching behind her, we're reminded that mountains are moved by carrying away small stones.

She smiles and proudly states: "I've just been relentless. It pays off."

---

10 As of 2020, this figure decreased to 2.3 percent during the COVID-19 pandemic.
    Source: https://hbr.org/2021/02/women-led-startups-received-just-2-3-of-vc-funding-in-2020
11 Source: https://www.womenspress.com/female-founders-on-the-rise

Papa Doble

"I have always had a soft spot for the Hemingway Daiquiri because of the grapefruit element and, in some cases, the Italian maraschino liqueur. My passion for artisan cocktails began in 1986, meaning I have tried a cocktail or two since then."

—Karen

Glass: Coupe
Garnish: Lime

1¾ oz. Montanya Platino
½ oz. lime juice
¾ oz. Luxardo maraschino liqueur
¾ oz. grapefruit juice
¼ oz. simple syrup

Add all ingredients to a mixing glass, shake with ice, and double strain into a coupe glass.

Kayla's Tip:
Some say this recipe requires no sugar, as the legendary boozehound was diabetic. Others say it requires double the amount of alcohol, as Papa usually ordered a double portion of rum. For a delicious drink, adjust your rum and sugar portions accordingly. To keep it classic, stay on the sour side.

DIY Tip:
To make simple syrup, combine one part white sugar with one part water by mass. Bring to a boil. Let cool before using.

Chapter 9

Magda López, Casa Botran, Guatemala

When you work in the rum industry, you learn to recognize the specific aromas and flavors that come with it. Therefore, it's not unusual to see rum lovers as devoted chefs, like our protagonist, Magda López, who sparks things up in the kitchen and Botran's aging facilities.

"The heat can bring up a lot of different flavors, just like charring the barrels," she laughs.

Working for Casa Botran in Guatemala for nearly thirty years, Magda knows the full range of flavors in rum, from notes of sugarcane to wooden casks. Given her fondness for flavor, it's not unusual to find her observing the aging process and the effect of different barrels, whether it's adding spicy or fruity aromas or even floral or vegetative notes.

"When I smell it, it takes me back to my childhood, when I first learned to recognize different flavors. I love what our brains make out of these elements. After all, there is no actual fruit in rum."

To Magda, it's fascinating how different types of barrels completely alter a taste profile. "You can achieve dramatically different results by burning the barrels on the inside (charring) or adjusting the aging period," she explains. "The fire can do a lot with the barrel. You can also create varieties within the concept, depending on how long you char it. For instance, you can toast the wood lightly or burn it until it cracks open and looks like alligator skin."

A young Magda (right) with her mother (center) and brother (left)

As Magda discusses the charring process, she lights up with joy. It all comes down to one thing: "Burning changes the smell of the barrel and therefore the rum." Playing with fire and keeping it under control must be challenging, but thanks to her knowledge and natural curiosity, Magda knows how to tame this wild element and produce a consistent, high-quality product each time.

Even as a little girl, Magda was curious about how food and drinks were made and read all the product labels. "I would study each ingredient and ask myself: how can I become part of this? How can I make it better?" she recalls.

Naturally, she went on to study the basis of everything: chemistry.

After completing her studies as a chemical engineer, Magda (right) attends graduation with her mother (left)

Before she could find her true calling at Botran, she needed experience. In her final year as a chemical engineer, an opportunity arose in the cosmetic industry, a seemingly obvious choice. After all, she wanted to develop new products, and she liked working with her nose, so why not perfume?

She felt this wasn't her final destination, though, and shortly after decided to travel to the US and study English. "I wanted a career at an international company, so I tried to prepare myself for it as best as possible," she reflects. "In a way, I created my own destiny."

As soon as she came back to Guatemala, she applied for a job in the spirits industry. "I wanted to diversify my experience, so I thought going from cosmetics to alcoholic drinks would help," she explains.

In 1991, she officially joined Botran's bottling facilities, where she worked at the company's quality control department. "I worked together with lab staff as I was supervising production. I found the process fascinating, and it sparked my curiosity for rum."

Two years later, she moved to Guatemala City to develop her skills under
Lorena Vasquez, her mentor at the time. During this time, Magda learned
to produce various beverages besides rum, like liqueurs and aguardiente,
another sugarcane-derived spirit. "I also helped develop the first batch
of ready-to-drink products, which was very interesting. I loved all this
diversity; it helped me grow," she tells us.

> Ready-to-drink (also known as RTD) are packaged beverages sold
> in a prepared form, ready for consumption. Examples include iced
> tea and alcopops, made by mixing alcoholic beverages with fruit
> juices or soft drinks.

One of the projects that Magda remembers fondly is Botran's Cafetto, a
delicious coffee liqueur. Guatemalan coffee is famous for its robust and
distinctive flavor, and mixing it with Guatemalan rum is a match made in
heaven. But as Magda always strives for the best, she couldn't settle for a
worthy-enough recipe.

**"I would study each ingredient and ask myself: how can I
become part of this? How can I make it better?"**

"I wanted to create an exceptional product, so I visited the coffee farms
and met the local producers. I noticed that the coffee tasted different
depending on which region it came from," she explains. "I decided to
blend different varieties and styles and came up with Cafetto's unique
taste profile. It remains one of my favorite creations today," she says with
a bright smile.

Magda poses with her family

Later, Magda moved to Quetzaltenango in the mountains, where she decided to explore Botran's aging facilities. The Solera system, a complex aging system involving multiple barrels and aged liquids, inspired her to try different production techniques and explore her creativity. "It fascinates me to see how the rum changes in a wooden barrel compared to a metal tank," she adds. "The only downside is I have to wait so long to taste the results!" (Botran's aging facilities are in the mountains, making the aging process even slower due to the lower temperatures.)

> "I tried to prepare myself for it as best as possible. In a way, I created my own destiny."

Becoming a master blender is like aging good rum. It takes time, patience, and expert knowledge. "If you want to do this, you need to learn about the entire company and appreciate the entire process from top to bottom," says Magda. "At Casa Botran, I wanted to know each product inside out, learn all about each stage of production, and discover new product characteristics."

Eventually, her curiosity bore fruit, and she became Botran's first female master blender in 2005.

Botran typically uses 200L ex-American whiskey barrels to age their rum. They may also use port and sherry barrels to achieve different taste profiles.

Even as a master blender, she still explores other departments and works closely with marketing to examine consumer trends and develop new products. "I love innovation, and I want to surprise our customers with something new and exciting," she says with a twinkle in her eye.

So far, Magda and her team have created various special edition rums, but her proudest achievement was made in 2012 when she was assigned to commemorate the end of the Mayan calendar.

"It was the end of an era, and many people even thought it would be the end of the world," she laughs. "To make this event more special and to celebrate my cultural heritage, I used white oak barrels made here in Guatemala. The spectrum of flavors was different from our standard range, with a long and unique finish."

Magda was also an integral part of Botran's commemorative seventy-fifth-anniversary gift set in 2015. "We wanted to allow customers to become 'master blenders' in their own homes," she explains.

This special set contains a 500ml bottle of Botran Gran Reserva matured in a Solera system for up to thirty years. "We used five different types of barrels in the system: port, sherry, two kinds of ex-American whiskey, and South American wine. Customers also got two small bottles of flavored rum, with initials B and C," she tells us. "The B version contained clove, nutmeg, and cinnamon notes, while the C version was on the citrus side, with accents of orange, grapefruit, and lime peel. All this was accompanied by a dropper, included to spark people's creativity and let them try their own blends."

Magda's innovative ideas are the driving force of the company. She feels lucky that her coworkers were generally supportive, although the beginning was tricky: "I was the only woman in the plant when I started thirty years ago, which felt very lonely. I didn't have any female peers until 1999, when the company started hiring more women in the lab. Our aging facilities consisted entirely of male workers until 2010, but this is changing now." As we speak, Magda is training two ladies that will become the next generation master blenders, Yasmin and Leslie.

As living proof that women can handle heat in the kitchen (and in the distillery)—it's just a question of time before a female-targeted rum hits the market. "Spirits producers have started to embrace female consumers and hire more female staff, which is great to see. About ten years ago, this position was almost exclusively held by men," she says. "It's great that we are more visible now. And I do hope this book will inspire more women to believe in their strengths and join us!"

Walking through the Casa Botran warehouse, Magda stops to show her latest creation.

Chirripeco Añejo

"I like to drink our Solera rum or the fifteen-year-old with just ice. Plain and simple. But I also like a cocktail with fruits and white rum. We have a Guatemala specialty: Chirripeco tea."

—Magda

This cocktail is specially made for Botran by Rodolfo Marroquín.

Glass: Coupe or martini
Garnish: Orange

1½ oz. Botran Añejo 18
¾ oz. vanilla syrup
3 oz. Chirripeco tea

Add all ingredients to a mixing glass, shake with ice, and double strain into a martini or coupe glass.

> **Kayla's Tip:**
> You can purchase vanilla syrup or make your own: Boil one part white sugar to one part water. Exposing the insides, add a vanilla pod. After five to ten minutes, remove from heat and strain.

> **Good to Know:**
> Chirrepeco Tea—from the Q'eqchi' "chirrepec," meaning "beside the cave"—is a traditional black tea grown by coop Alta Verapaz in San Juan Chamelco, Guatemala. If unavailable, substitute with black tea.

Chapter 10

Jassil Villanueva, Brugal, Dominican Republic

Some rum distilleries are family-owned, so the responsibilities of a master blender are handed down through generations. This is the case for Brugal, a premium rum brand founded in 1888 by Don Andrés Brugal Montaner in the Dominican Republic. Traditionally, only male family members were allowed to become the *maestro ronero*, Spanish for rum master. However, five generations later, Brugal opened its ranks to the first woman in its history, Jassil Villanueva. Not only is she the first *maestra ronera* in the Dominican Republic, but she's also the youngest person to receive that prestigious title at just twenty-eight years old.

Jassil is honored and proud to take over such a big responsibility, having watched her father and uncles cultivate the tradition for over twenty-five years. She never doubted she would join the family business eventually, though at first, she was more interested in operations than making rum.

"I first visited the distillery with my dad when I was five or six and was immediately fascinated by the inner workings of the warehouse. Later, I would regularly visit to be part of it," she recalls. "There are so many people working behind the brand, even doing small manual tasks like sticking labels on bottles. Our visitors love to see that, just like I did when I was a kid. It's so amazing to witness the entire process."

When she grew up, Jassil got her MBA and relocated to the US to practice her English. Still, she remained close to her family in Puerto Plata and even completed an internship at the company during her college years. "I just couldn't wait to return and get into the real world," she says. "My education served me as a good base to start, but I had no idea I was going to become a rum master.

Everything changed when she received an invitation to the trials for the fifth-generation master blender.

"Every few years, my family organizes a sort of competition, looking for new blood and new talents," she explains. "And for the first time in the history of Brugal, they decided to invite a woman as well."

As Jassil tells us, you can't simply apply for this position as an outsider. You need to be a descendant of founder Andrés Brugal Montaner and devoted to the family business. Out of eleven applicants, she was the only woman and the youngest in the group. "It was a bit scary, but I like to take opportunities when they arise."

After a year of evaluations, the rum masters decided Jassil was to become the first *maestra ronera*.

Jassil inspects barrels at the Brugal warehouse.

"In the Dominican Republic, people weren't used to seeing ladies drinking spirits—this was unthinkable only a decade ago," she adds.

She recalls that though her family was very protective of her, at the same time, their expectations were high. "All eyes were on me to see how things would turn out," she says. "Nobody thought a lady would get the job, and everyone knew me as my dad's little girl, so they were worried about me. Fortunately, I work better under pressure," she laughs.

Being selected as the future master blender is only the first step. What follows is years of rigorous training and honing of sensory skills. Jassil also had to work in other departments to learn about each step of the production process.

"My first job was to be a brand ambassador, which taught me all about our products," she tells us. "Then, I moved on to other areas. It's one thing to see these departments work in front of you, but actually doing the job made me understand the entire process a lot better."

After three years of training in various departments, Jassil was finally ready to start making rum.

"...everyone knew me as my dad's little girl, so they were worried about me. Fortunately, I work better under pressure."

At any given moment, Brugal has a few master blenders with varied responsibilities. Jassil works with four others from the fourth generation and three from the fifth.

Before tasting the rum, Jassil gently noses the glass.

"When you're part of the family, you get to look after a specific task," she explains. "For instance, some rum masters are in charge of the formulation; others look after projects or engineering."

Jassil's responsibility is to oversee the aging process and develop new products, both significant contributions. However, she finds her age as the most challenging aspect of her job. "At the beginning, I felt like a small kid, a bit out of place," she recalls. "I felt like people would judge me because I was so young. Most people think you can't have this specific knowledge and experience unless you're an older person."

Still, despite the initial skepticism, Jassil has settled in well into her new role: "When you have the joy and passion for what you're doing, everything else is just not important. And with time, I was no longer seen as daddy's little girl; instead, he was the father of the *maestra ronera*."

With everyone so protective of Jassil, working in the Dominican Republic felt like a bubble. But traveling to Europe came with different roadblocks.

"Back home, everyone knew me, but abroad, this wasn't the case," she explains. "People were not used to women leading masterclasses and teaching men how to taste or what not to do." This made her realize that the rum industry is still not fully embracing women, but it didn't discourage her.

"It made me want to try harder and infect everyone with my passion. I wanted to bring them to the same level of energy and fun. And I'm excited to lead the new generation of women in the rum industry and prove that there's nothing we can't do."

"With time, I was no longer seen as daddy's little girl; instead, he was the father of the *maestra ronera*."

Jassil is optimistic about the future of rum, with the general perception changing around this spirit.

"Consumers expect more from their drinks," she tells us. "They want to find new expressions and specific notes. People don't just want a drink; they want to enjoy it. Premium rum has more feminine qualities as it's more elegant and detailed, which consumers appreciate."

For an elevated experience, pour Brugal over a large ice sphere. Enjoy.

Her proudest moment at Brugal was crafting the limited-edition Papa Andres blend. "The rum has existed for a while, but it was reserved for special family occasions like reunions," she explains. "In 2013, we released a commercial edition for the first time. I created the second edition (2015), and it was a huge honor. It surpassed everyone's expectations, and nobody knew who made it or that the creator was a woman."

As Brugal is part of the Edrington Group, home to several Scottish malt whisky brands, Jassil compares current customer trends with her fellow female whisky makers. "We share our knowledge and exchange experiences because, even though we make different spirits, we encounter similar professional challenges."

The Edrington Group was founded in 1961 by the Robertson sisters (Elspeth, Agnes, and Ethel), who inherited the Scotch whisky interests developed by their grandfather and father. Keen to ensure the welfare of their employees and support good causes in Scotland, the sisters established a registered charity, providing financial support to school children and students from deprived backgrounds. Brugal has been part of the Edrington Group since 2008.

As more and more women join the spirits industry, the rum world looks more joyful than ever before.

Elspeth, Agnes, and Ethel

"To me, the rum scene is one of the happiest worlds there is, and ladies have this natural instinct to create joyful moments." She then adds, "Don't be afraid to try many different things; you never know where it might lead. The spirits world allows you to use your creativity, and it can be such a joyful place. I can't wait for other women to join."

Coconut Ice Ball

"This cocktail was inspired by Brugal's fourth Generation Maestro Ronero Don Fernando 'Nano' José Ortega. The subtle sweetness and natural flavors of the coconut infuse nicely with the rum. For me, it's a perfect combination because you don't have to do a lot of work to get a delicious drink."

—Jassil

Glass: Rocks
Garnish: Lime peel

Put ice in the shaker
1½ oz. Brugal 1888 Doblemente Añejado
Dash of lime
Ice ball of frozen coconut water

Add ice ball to a rocks glass. Pour rum and lime over ball. Stir to dilute.

Kayla's Tip:
The ice ball will slowly melt, making each sip different from the previous one. Go too fast, and you won't taste much coconut, but sip too slow, and it'll overwhelm the rum. Pacing yourself here is crucial.

DIY Tip:
To make a coconut ice ball, fill a sphere mold with coconut water and freeze. If this cocktail is too spirit-forward, add simple syrup or let the ice melt into the drink.

Chapter 11

Karine Lassalle, Rhum J.M, Martinique

As we connect with Karine Lassalle, quality control manager and cellar master at Rhum J.M in Martinique, we can't help but admire the landscape behind her.

"It's a beautiful island," she agrees. "I fell in love with the exotic aromas in the air as soon as I landed here. That's when I knew rum was my destiny. It's the ultimate tropical *joie de vivre*."

Originally from Maubourguet, France, Karine grew up in the southwestern countryside. Her family always appreciated the local produce, and with famous wineries nearby, they would usually have a stock of classic Bordeaux or Madiran in the house. "My grandpa would even rinse his plate with a bit of wine. He claimed it was to clean the remains of the soup, but really, he just wanted a sip of wine," she laughs.

Karine's parents would also have a personal reserve of Armagnac, a type of brandy from a French area north of Maubourguet. "Of course, I never had any alcohol as a child, but one of my fondest memories was coming down to the family cellar with that lovely Armagnac scent mixed with my father's cigar. It was so comforting," she recalls.

Coming from a home with such a strong tradition for French wine and brandy, it comes as little surprise that Karine found a career in the spirits industry. However, she originally envisaged a different path for herself. "I was always fascinated with perfume," she tells us, "I wanted to be the *nose* in the business." To make her dreams a reality, she pursued a degree in chemistry with a specialty in perfumes at the University of Montpellier.

A nose is a term used to describe a perfume artist. This person is typically responsible for portraying moods, emotions, and concepts through fragrance composition.

Her olfactory talents were quickly noticed by Jean Lenoir, the esteemed creator of Le Nez du Vin (The Nose of Wine), a collection of aromas that characterize different wines. He offered to work with her on the next big project: an inventory of smells commonly found in whisky. She decided to take the opportunity and helped create Le Nez du Whisky, an educational set with fifty-four aromas that make up the DNA of this spirit.

"Creating these scents took me back to my childhood. My family were carpenters, and my father dried wood in a kiln before working on it. I used to go with him to check and regulate the temperature and humidity of the room. I loved that smell of damp wood, and today, it follows me in my work in our cellars," she smiles as her memories come alive once again. "This job introduced me to the sentimental aromas of whisky, and later, rum. I had to explore it and see where it led."

Before pursuing the art of spirits, a young Karine dabbled in the art of ballet.

Working on a high-profile project like Le Nez du Whisky was a perfect
business card. But it was her trip to Martinique that made her realize that
she wanted to make rum, not whisky. "I visited the Clement distillery, and
I immediately fell in love with the surrounding scent. I was also amazed to
discover the full range of flavors and luscious aromas in rum," she recalls.

When asked whether she finds rum superior to whisky, she tells us: "It's
a matter of preference. Just like my grandfather preferred Armagnac
above cognac, I prefer rum over whisky. Besides, I love the sunny
Caribbean weather; whisky-producing countries like Scotland are a bit
too rainy," she says.

Her short holiday in Martinique turned out to be another defining
moment. That's when Karine set a new goal for herself: to come back and
work in a rum distillery. A few years later, she accomplished her dream,
working for brands like Distillerie du Simon and Rhum HSE. Together,
they helped her gain the necessary experience and know-how about
rhum agricole.

"I fell in love with the exotic aromas in the air as soon as I landed here. That's when I knew rum was my destiny. It's the ultimate tropical *joie de vivre*."

In 2017, she joined J.M as a cellar master (*maître de chai*), a title typically used in the context of wine. It also describes the person responsible for the development and aging of rum in French-speaking areas. Holding such a senior position at the age of thirty-one was an outstanding achievement, but it also came with some challenges.

"I came there as a young French woman to continue the tradition of Martiniquan rum and supervise a team of Martiniquan men. Most of them worked there for decades, so they challenged and tested my knowledge, making the first few months intense," she recalls.

"I explained I wasn't there to teach them how to make rum. I was there to work together as a team, to make the highest quality product. I assured them my goal was not to change it but to improve it," she said. On reflection, she understands their resistance. "I was new. I stepped into their 'male' world as a woman, and I had quite some shoes to fill. My predecessor, Nazaire Canatous, worked there for over forty years."

Before joining J.M, Karine begins her rum journey at Rhum HSE.

As humble as she is about her position in the company, her expertise, perseverance, and go-getter attitude quickly established her as the perfect leader. "I don't want to dwell in negativity. I look for solutions instead. My strategy worked, and six months later, I was fully accepted in the team," she reflects.

Despite the challenges women encounter when entering a male-dominated industry, Karine believes that the rum world is open to female professionals. "I think we are often afraid to pursue jobs in fields that are considered male because we see it as a man's world, and we doubt whether we can match the skills. Of course, we can. We need to step up and just go for it. Be courageous. Be the role model for future women," she says.

Asked about her influences, she mentions Joy Spence of Appleton Estate in Jamaica. "My dream is to meet her and ask what she thinks about my rum," she smiles.

Veteran employees are awarded medals for their contributions to Rhum J.M. From left to right: Karine, cooper Edmond Lina, cellar master Nazaire Canatous, cooper Alain Malle, cooper Yannick Defrel

Karine believes the spirits industry is in a transitional phase. "Being a cellar master is a life-long job, so many male rum producers will soon retire. A certain era is ending. More and more companies are open to the idea that women have the necessary skills to make good rum. Now is our time to take their places and create a new future, or someone else will," she says.

Not only does she champion inclusivity, she also advocates for sustainability and ethical rum production. Because she grew up in the countryside, the love for the environment runs in her blood. "We grew our own vegetables, caught fish, and harvested mushrooms. We also did our best to reduce waste and respect nature," she recalls.

She proudly reports that J.M focuses on eco-responsibility at every stage of production, from distilling to bottling. For one, they use their own bagasse (dried sugarcane leftovers) in their heating system. Karine also avoids additives and aims to keep rum as pure as possible: "We need to take care of nature and take care of ourselves, too."

But for Karine, producing pure rum is more than just avoiding additives like caramel; it's a holistic approach. "To take care of the rum means to take care of the casks," she says. "I want to cultivate the spirit of Martinique with this rum and give our consumers that 'I want to go back' moment."

Since joining, J.M expanded their facilities by adding two new cellars, which allowed Karine to add her twist while retaining the traditional recipe. As we speak, she's working on her own creation: "Rum offers innovation, and there's a lot of room for creativity, which is important for me."

Looking back at her short time with J.M, Karine is proud of the successful handover between her and the previous cellar master, Nazaire. "He observed me a lot and quickly understood that I had the respect for the old. That's when he serenely passed on the solid foundations to ensure the continuity of the brand and meet the expectations of the customers," she says. Asked about unpleasant experiences, she assures us there were none.

Wrapping up, we have to return to the French philosophy of *joie de vivre*, the joy of living, and how it connects to rum.

"To me, rum is pure joy, and living on a tropical island connects me with nature, which makes me happy," she explains. "I truly believe in this philosophy and try to appreciate my surroundings, the people around me, and grab each opportunity that presents itself. We only have one life."

Surrounded by casks, Karine and Nazaire Canatous chat in the Rhum J.M warehouse.

The essence of Martiniquan *joie de vivre* is perhaps best contained in the way the locals say goodbye, which Karine tells us is *I'll see you tomorrow if God allows it*. We sure hope we will!

"To me, rum is pure joy."

Agric'old Fashioned

"One of my favorite cocktails, and it doesn't take more than that to please me! The VSOP is a four-year-old rum with luscious flavors of exotic fruits and complex roasted notes that blend perfectly with our Shrubb. This liqueur is a tradition in Martinique and is often prepared traditionally in every family for the Christmas period."

—Karine

Glass: Rocks
Garnish: Orange peel

2 oz. J.M VSOP
½ oz. Shrubb J.M
3 drops of Angostura bitters

Add all ingredients to a mixing glass, stir with ice, and strain over clean ice (rocks or one big cube) into a rocks glass.

DIY Tip:
When slicing your orange peel, avoid the pith.

Good to Know:
When cocktails took off in the late 1800s, drinks started getting too "complex." People preferred the "old fashioned" serve—a base spirit, a touch of sugar, and a few dashes of bitters."

Chapter 12

Sharon Sue-Hang, Demerara Distillers Ltd., Guyana

Female rum leaders are fearless and unapologetic in reaching their goals in a male-dominated industry. Sharon Sue-Hang, the master blender of Demerara Distillers Ltd. (DDL) in Guyana, is no different, and she believes nothing is unachievable. "You might fall along the way, but then you just get up, brush yourself off, and go again," she says.

Indeed, Sharon is an inspiring role model and a champion for science and education, paving the way for future female leaders in Guyana and beyond.

Sharon was born in New Amsterdam, a small town in the county of Berbice, Guyana. For as long as she can remember, she has been fascinated with science. "Unfortunately, I couldn't deal with certain medical conditions, so becoming a medical doctor was out of the question," she laughs. "Chemistry was a natural fit for me. I always loved conducting experiments in high school."

She later relocated to Georgetown to attend the University of Guyana, where she got her bachelor of science in chemistry. She never returned to her hometown as her dream career was waiting around the corner.

While pursuing her degree, Sharon pictured herself in the pharmaceutical industry rather than behind the stills. "For sure, I wasn't thinking of a career in rum at that age," she says. "I didn't even drink until I was in my early twenties. After becoming familiar with the product and its diverse flavors, I knew that I wanted to use my skills to produce rums with wide flavor profiles."

"You might fall along the way, but then you just get up, brush yourself off, and go again."

To this day, she stays faithful to the classical Demerara taste profile, with robust, peaty, tarry notes that she enjoys the most. On reflection, Sharon thinks she always displayed more sensitivity to flavors than others. However, it wasn't until she started working at DDL that she truly understood the nuances and different taste profiles in rum.

Sharon operates a now obsolete desktop computer.

As a fresh graduate, she started looking out for jobs in the area. Her excellent student records attracted several interviews. "With my skill set, I applied mainly to manufacturing companies, but the one that particularly sparked my interest was the rum distillery," she explains.

So in 1995, she officially joined the quality assurance department at DDL, producer of the renowned El Dorado rums.

Although Sharon had no practical experience, DDL provided an excellent training program that still runs today. "We take university graduates from different fields and put them on a one-year management trainee program," she explains. "I started as a management trainee chemist and got moved around various manufacturing areas, learning about all aspects of the work. Then, after a year, trainees get evaluated to see if they're a good fit for the company."

Nowadays, DDL still employs their best chemists through that program, allowing talented graduates to gain experience and move up the ladder.

In the quality control department, part of her on-the-job training was to perform a sensory evaluation. However, Sharon tells us it's not enough to understand chemistry to evolve in this job; one also needs excellent nosing and tasting skills.

"Some days, I would work alongside people who weren't able to differentiate between various liquids while I could immediately pick up the differences," she explains. "It was during the organoleptic assessments that my supervisors noticed my qualities and invited me to join the official tasting panel."

Sharon got to blind taste the finished liquids just before they hit the market, a testament to her sensory skills. "I had to know what to look for, understand different profiles, and reference various flavors," she explains. Back then, she was the only woman on the panel and one of the few female chemists in the company.

On his 2000 visit to Demerara Distillers, His Royal Highness Prince Charles (right) noses a bottle alongside Sharon

Sharon also got to work alongside back-then master distiller George Leslie Robinson, or GLR as he was fondly known. He was in the business for more than forty years, and to all who worked with him, he was the ultimate mentor. "When he suddenly passed away in 2011, somebody had to come forward to take over his tasks," she recalls.

That person was Sharon, who had to step into GLR's shoes without a proper handover. "It's a job that carries a lot of responsibilities on its shoulders, and sometimes your shoulders aren't broad enough," she explains. "But I was excited about the opportunity."

With the arrival of a new master blender, it was time to introduce some innovations. "I maintained the older blends but also worked on some new ones," she explains. "I can get creative with the rum because the stills are versatile, and they can produce various styles and products."

Currently, DDL has fourteen different stills, most of which come from distilleries that were shut down decades ago. Each has a distinct influence on the spirit, giving Sharon a wide range of taste profiles to work with when creating new blends. "I love making new products that people will enjoy when the bottles finally land in the shops," she tells us.

"It's a job that carries a lot of responsibilities on its shoulders, and sometimes your shoulders aren't broad enough."

But, of course, a three-hundred-year-old brand needs to retain tradition where possible. Lucky for Sharon, she loves diversity.

Changes in the workplace are never easy, and Sharon was no exception. "People were generally supportive, but there was a bit of resistance at first, especially when someone did things differently for many years," she reflects. "I had to explain why my way would be more valuable and beneficial."

Reflecting on why there are still not that many women working in distilleries, she feels that manufacturing jobs are often physical. "I've been seeing more women in the field than when I first started," she says. "But traditionally, working in a factory setting is seen as hard work. It may look unachievable or off-putting to some. Now that females are becoming more visible in the distilling industry, younger women can see them and think, *Hey, if she can climb up there, I could do that too.*"

Being among few females back when she started, her advice to future women in the industry is to work toward their dream and never give up. "Make sure to understand the role, equip yourself with the right knowledge, and work toward that. Be diligent and determined because if you persevere, you will get there."

But Sharon knows that perseverance can only get you so far and feels that access to education is critical if we want to see changes in the world. She is an active member of several charitable organizations, including

Rotary International, which promotes literacy. "I help kids who are not able to be in school or maybe don't do well due to limited access to resources," she explains. "I'm also part of the DDL Foundation, which offers financial backing for students who can't afford higher education."

While testing a new barrel, Sharon measures out a sample.

She also feels strongly about the inclusion of women into the STEM disciplines (science, technology, engineering, mathematics). "Many people believe that only boys can do well in these fields, so girls shy away from them," she tells us. "But females can excel in these subjects too. We need more scientists in the world to cure diseases or develop vaccines."

Of course, rum is a special niche, combining science and creativity, and the industry can only benefit from men's and women's unique talents. "Women see things differently, for sure. And we have finesse in doing things."

"Now that females are becoming more visible in the distilling industry, younger women can see them and think, *Hey, if she can climb up there, I could do that too.*"

So what is next for Sharon? Certainly, she will continue to innovate and exceed DDL's customer expectations, though she remains humble.

At the DDL warehouse, Sharon noses a glass.

"I'm not a genius; I just listen to what our consumers are saying, and I translate it into a product."

Mojito

"If I am with friends, I drink the five-year-old with coconut water. It is straightforward but really, really refreshing and delicious."

—Sharon

Glass: Collins
Garnish: Slap a mint spring on the back of your hand to activate aromas and garnish. Serve with a straw or mixing stick.

6 mint leaves
½ oz. simple syrup
1 oz. lime juice
2 oz. El Dorado 3 yrs.
Splash of soda water

Muddle mint, simple syrup, and lime juice in a strong glass. Add ice and churn well with a bar spoon to disperse mint, mix, and dilute your drink. Top with fresh ice to the top of the glass, then soda water.

Kayla's Tip:
When muddling mint, bruise it enough to activate the aromas. For a refreshing flavor, use cracked or crushed ice and a dash of bitters.

DIY Tip:
To make simple syrup, boil one part white sugar with one part water.

Chapter 13

Salomé Alemán Carriazo, Havana Club, Cuba

Being the forerunner and leader in your field comes with many responsibilities. For Salomé Alemán Carriazo, master blender of Havana Club, it's not just cultivating the Cuban rum tradition. It's also championing other women in the industry, advocating for better inclusivity, and fighting against ageism in the workplace. She firmly believes that diversity can strengthen any company and that your gender, age, or background shouldn't matter if you have the necessary knowledge, skills, and passion for your job.

Salomé assures us her upbringing had nothing to do with rum. Growing up in boisterous Havana, her childhood was calm, and as she entered adulthood, the thought of working with spirits never occurred to her. Instead, she was interested in science, and in 1988, she enrolled in the University of Technical Sciences (CUJAE) to pursue engineering and chemistry.

Her junior year, she interned at the Santa Cruz distillery and came across rum for the first time. The place was beautiful and the atmosphere alluring. Her internship was short, but it was enough to familiarize her with the famed Havana Club and offer practical experience as a chemical engineer. After that, she knew she wanted to go back.

> The Santa Cruz distillery is the largest rum factory in Cuba and belongs to the Cuba Ron S.A. Corporation, located in Santa Cruz del Norte, 50 km east of the capital.

When she graduated, Salomé returned to the Santa Cruz distillery. "My only ambition was to acquire all the knowledge I could and keep developing as a professional," she recalls. "My initial plan was to stay in the company for two years and move on, but I never left."

She never thought she would become a master blender, but her skills didn't go unnoticed. "The master blender culture is a peculiar one in Cuba, and I didn't fully understand what it meant back then," she explains. "My only ambition was to become very good at my job. My performance was so good that the senior rum master proposed me as a candidate for this role."

> "Master blender" has different terminology depending on the world region and distillery. For example, in Cuba, this function is called the master of rum (maestro del ron), and the headmaster blender is called the first rum master (gran maestro del ron).

Rum master training took six years, but Salomé only remembers it as a beautiful experience. During this time, she was trained by her mentor and First Master of Cuban Rum, Juan Carlos Gonzáles Delgado, and other rum masters within the company.

Salomé contemplates which sample to try first.

"I experienced the full cycle of production, from the raw ingredients to the finished rum," she explains. "I had to rotate between all the jobs in the distillery and see firsthand what happened at every step of the process."

Salomé officially became master of rum on May 24, 2016, and the first woman to hold the title in Cuba. "I felt privileged because I had completed my rigorous training in the factory. This was the highest professional recognition that a technician in the world of spirits could have," she tells us.

As beautiful as it was to become the first female rum master, she was both excited and scared. From the moment she started her new position and joined the team, her life changed radically. She began to understand the culture behind her work and the great responsibility that came with it.

"In Cuba, we do not take any formal course to become a rum master. Instead, we learn from the hands-on experiences of older people... All rum masters work as a team, one that is responsible for our national cultural heritage. Therefore, each person has to embody virtues and values. Of course, we had many things in common on a professional level, but I also introduced a feminine vision, which was hard for some people to accept."

She believes that women, in general, have a natural ability to reach their goals without conflicting with others in the group. The training she received helped her gain respect, but it also taught her about self-respect. "I think the hardest thing was to become integrated without imposing my beliefs on them too much. I had to demonstrate skills and abilities instead of just strength. This way, I could build a good image as a professional, but also as a person. I consider that to be my personal business card," she says.

"All rum masters work as a team, one that is responsible for our national cultural heritage. Therefore, each person has to embody virtues and values."

As she grew into her role as the first female rum master in the company, Salomé also developed a significant role for other women in the island's spirits industry. "Our rum scene was, just like everywhere else, male-dominated, but I disrupted that image," she says.

At Havana Club's San José distillery, Salomé swirls her glass and checks the coloring.

She set an example for women in other economic sectors and decided to participate in actions for greater integration and cooperation with women of all age groups. "I want to see more teams where gender or age don't matter, and it's particularly tough for women who reach a certain age."

When it comes to the intersection of gender and age, parenthood and the lack of accommodation for caregivers often hinder inclusivity— an obstacle women continue to overcome. "As women, nature has given us the gift of motherhood. But the fact that we have been able to get integrated into the working society without neglecting our responsibilities as mothers is very encouraging. It shows other women that it can be done."

However, it's clear to Salomé that more work is still to be done.

Salomé brings a barrel into her office.

She stresses the social impact of integrating women into the rum world and the potential domino effect it would bring. "Hiring more women in key production roles contributes to the social inclusion of women, showing that they contribute to the economy. When women achieve success in a particular sector, it has a huge impact on the image of women in general in our society. It's like a drop of water in a lake that expands more and more, and the rum industry could be that drop." She adds: "Whenever a woman is integrated into a male-dominated scene, that means the world is ready for more."

Daiquiri

"I love this classic cocktail. It usually is with unaged rum, but I love it with the three years old. That rum is produced in my distillery (Havana Club has several), and I have devoted practically my whole professional life to this product."

—Salomé

Glass: Coupe
Garnish: A wedge of lime

2 oz. Havana Club 3 yrs.
1 oz. lime juice
½ oz. simple syrup

Add all ingredients to a mixing glass, shake with ice, and double strain into a coupe glass.

Kayla's Tip:
A lighter rum, be it unaged or aged and filtered, will yield that classic pale, almost glowing effect we so lovingly associate with the daiquiri. While many claim a daiquiri is made with "white" or "silver" rum, you can use any rum you wish.

DIY Tip:
To make simple syrup, combine one part white sugar with one part water by mass. Bring to a boil in a pot. Let cool before using. Store in the fridge for up to a month.

Chapter 14

Silvia Santiago, Don Q, Puerto Rico

Silvia Santiago, the master blender of Don Q rums, is not afraid to ask questions or step out of her comfort zone. Always hungry for knowledge, Silvia's philosophy is simple: try everything and never say no to a new opportunity. This is how she grew in her career: from microbiologist to *maestra ronera*, Silvia now runs the entire operation at Destilería Serrallés.

Silvia was born and raised in the historic parts of Ponce, Puerto Rico. As she describes it, her parents came from humble roots. "My father went to the army because there weren't many jobs here," she tells us. "My mother raised us with very little money. She made miracles and encouraged us to study, our cheerleader every step of the way."

Silvia always dreamt of going to college, but her family couldn't afford it. So, when she received a letter from the local university offering a scholarship, it was a dream come true. "I was so happy. It was my motivation to do my best."

She completed her degree in medical technology in just four years, a path that typically takes five years or more. She was equal parts eager and dedicated; she would start her courses early in the summertime and study until late at night. She enrolled in all possible classes and wanted to take full advantage of her scholarship.

Silvia was always inclined toward the sciences and decided to pursue this direction. "I remember I wanted to become an astronaut as a little girl," she tells us. "But when I started studying, I got interested in chemistry and microbiology." Somewhere along the way, she interned in hospitals, drawing blood from patients. "I liked it; it added a human factor to the job, and I could help people," she says.

Once she finished university, she had plans to continue working at hospitals, but a different opportunity came along. "There was this distillery looking for a person who could work with yeast," she recalls. "They came to my university, interviewed a few people, and chose me."

The company turned out to be Destilería Serrallés, producer of the renowned Don Q rums. As Silvia tells us, the company was so impressed with her that they agreed to wait three months until she finished her degree. "I graduated on Friday and started my first day the following Monday," she laughs.

Destilería Serrallés is best known for its Don Q rum brand. The company is Puerto Rico's oldest family-owned company, established in the 1860s by Don Juan Serrallés. The Serrallés family originated from Catalonia, Spain, and their sugar cane plantation virtually became a company town with its own rail line and later even an airport (Ponce's Mercedita Airport).

This was an entirely different scenario for her; she had no idea where this career could lead, but the change excited her. "I remember my first day; I immediately fell in love with the smell of molasses," she recalls. "After forty-seven years, I still wake up in the morning and feel the same joy as the day I started. I am blessed in that sense."

The Serrallés family

As soon as she joined the company, Silvia wanted to learn everything about the production process. She noticed her colleagues were protective about their responsibilities, but she was never afraid to ask questions. "I was very curious, and because I was so young, I wasn't a threat," she explains. The engineers even made drawings to illustrate how the plant worked. "Everyone was willing to explain things to me. I tried to learn something new every day."

Eventually, Silvia knew enough about distillation to put her ideas forward, though her colleagues weren't always receptive. "I'm guided by science, but also my intuition, which men don't always understand," she tells us. Still, Silvia was eager to expand her knowledge and take on new responsibilities.

"I never said no because I didn't know how to do it," she explains. "Sometimes we want to wait until we know how to do something, but that doesn't always work. We have to stretch ourselves; that's how we grow."

Thanks to her curiosity, Silvia learned all about the production process in a short time, but one puzzle piece was missing—she wanted to understand the nuances between aromas and flavors.

"I became fascinated by the sensory tasting," she tells us. "But this task was reserved for a man the staff called 'The Cuban.' He would always go to a special room to perform his analysis, and he would throw out whoever would attempt to go with him," she laughs.

As she watched this mysterious colleague—Don Q's master blender, Adolfo Torres, at the time—Silvia grew more curious about his work. "Back then, I had no idea how it was done, so I began approaching this man. To my amazement, he answered my questions and started giving me different samples to smell."

"Sometimes we want to wait until we know how to do something, but that doesn't always work. We have to stretch ourselves; that's how we grow."

Silvia had an excellent understanding of chemistry and a sensitive nose, which didn't go unnoticed by Adolfo, who eventually started mentoring her. "I think he always knew that I could do that job," she tells us. "One time, he asked me to smell different samples of water, explaining he was looking for a good source for production. One of the samples smelled like rotten eggs. I knew it smelled bad because of the sulfur elements, but he didn't know that much about chemistry. Still, he could detect it in parts per billion because he was so experienced."

Silvia tells us that one can develop sensory skills with diligent practice, though she believes women have an extra edge. "We have to take care of our children and do things at home, so all our senses are working at the same time," she laughs.

Handwritten formulas and notes of the Serrallés family.

Eventually, Silvia became part of a team that regularly evaluated new blends, and soon a new opportunity would present itself. One day, her mentor handed her the keys to the tasting room and said, "You'll be doing this from now on."

The tasting room soon became Silvia's sacred shrine, where she could sit down and think about her work. Now, Silvia doesn't believe in ghosts, but she admits she felt something the moment she entered that room. "We are all energy; we're surrounded by it," she explains. "Whenever I work there, I do it with so much respect. When I read those handwritten notes of my predecessors from many years ago or handle formulas that only family members were allowed to touch, I feel their energy is still there. It's so special, and I feel honored to be part of that legacy."

But Silvia isn't the only one sensing this legacy. Within the last years, rum has been gaining more recognition in the spirits world. With this rum renaissance, rum has gone from a simple beach drink with an ungrateful reputation to a refined spirit. "Rum has a lot of history, technology, and craft," she explains. "It has character and can be very robust, especially aged rum. So, it deserves proper space around the world, like whisky and cognac."

At the Don Q lab, Silvia identifies aromas with her nose.

Workers in rum productions see the spirit as not just part of their jobs but as a serious part of their lives. For one, Silvia spends her free time visiting other distilleries and learning about their processes. Of course, some producers will never reveal their secrets, but her keen sense of smell can pick up subtle nuances (such as different molasses).

According to Silvia, Don Q now has a computerized distillation control system. This helps Silvia and the team remain consistent and improve the process without changing any of the elements. They still pasteurize the molasses the same way as before (pasteurization kills wild yeast and bacteria, preventing spoiling and unwanted flavors). Even a small change in the process can have huge consequences on the outcome, which is why consistency is so important in rum production.

At work, she strives to improve Don Q's operations while maintaining the traditional taste. This comes easy when you're confident in the quality of your products and your excellent team.

"We take great care of each stage of the process, from molasses to fermentation and beyond," she explains. "We now have several ladies in the operations area, and there's also a female master distiller. She's an engineer with a lot of knowledge. I can tell her there's a certain problem with a sample, and fifteen minutes later, she comes back with a solution."

Silvia checks a bottle of Don Q 7.

With female producers gaining more visibility, industries will eventually become more diverse, eliminating problems Silvia encountered in her early years. "When I started, I was the only woman in the entire production area, not just the laboratory," she explains. "I never experienced any hostility, but sometimes it felt like I wasn't part of the group." Later, she adds: "One time I was giving a seminar, and a man came up to me and said: 'Wow, I never thought a woman could do that.'"

It turns out a woman can. And in Silvia's case, it all started with a simple question. "Don't stop yourself; challenge yourself. Learning will open doors, and from there, you only need to step through."

Curiosity doesn't seem to always kill the cat. Sometimes, it just makes really good rum.

Honey Breeze

"I really had to think about it. If I name a cocktail, I want it to make me feel I am on the beach, watching a beautiful sunset. A nice big glass with a straw in my hand and enjoying life. A not-too-complicated cocktail with fresh ingredients. A slight breeze to cool us down a bit."

—Silvia

Glass: Highball or tiki mug
Garnish: Cucumber

2 oz. Don Q Reserva 7 yrs.
¼ oz. honey syrup
2 oz. coconut water
2 cm cucumber

Muddle the cucumber in the mixing glass. Add ingredients and ice. Shake, single strain into a highball glass or tiki mug filled with ice. Double strain to remove any cucumber chunks.

Kayla's Tip:
Use a large glass or crushed ice and make sure the ice pokes above the liquid. To make homemade honey syrup, mix two parts honey with one part water. Bring to a boil.

Good to Know:
An ancient Maori myth tells of Tiki, the first man. Inspired by the sentimental appeal of an idealized South Pacific, tiki culture popped up in 1930s California and spread around the world.

Chapter 15

Maggie Campbell, Independent Consultant[12], USA

Like most other female rum makers in this book, Maggie Campbell unexpectedly entered the rum world. A philosophy graduate, product developer, business strategist, aspiring Wine Master, beekeeper, and inspirational TEDx speaker, Maggie defies all labels and, as she calls it, craves to soak up knowledge. She believes in the art of *élevage*, a French term that describes the betterment of wine. She applies it not only in rum production but also in personal life, striving for continuous development.

Maggie's journey began during her university years. Intending to explore her family roots, she traveled to Oban in the Scottish Highlands and booked a ferry to the Isle of Mull. With a few hours to kill before her trip, she decided to visit the local whisky distillery, an experience that opened the window to a whole new universe. "I saw people working in their overalls and boots, which felt familiar to me as my father was a truck driver. That's when I first thought that, maybe, this is something that I could do," she recalls.

---

12 Maggie was acting as an independent rum consultant at the time of our interview. In October 2021, she joined Mount Gay as their new Estate Rum Manager.

A young Maggie rides horseback.

When she graduated with her philosophy degree, Maggie struggled to find job opportunities, especially in her field. With the 2008 economic crash looming, she enrolled in some wine classes to learn about technical tasting. The course taught her about fermentation, differentiating between barrels and grapes, and recognizing top-quality wine—skills that would impact her distilling style later on. Soon after, she got a job as a wine specialist at a local liquor store.

At the time, the economic crash was leading people to empty their cellars. "I got to handle some really fine wine and met collectors from the scene," she recalls. "I also noticed customers had a growing interest in spirits. It's around the time the show *Mad Men* first started airing. I was the only person at the store who had any distillation knowledge, which made me realize I had an edge."

Colorado has relatively friendly laws concerning alcohol production, so it's no wonder it became home to the second wave of the American craft distillation movement in the 2000s (with the first one happening in the '90s). Over a decade later, Maggie is at the forefront of the third wave.

The American Craft Spirits Association defines a craft distillery as follows: *A distillery that values the importance of transparency in distilling, and remains forthcoming regarding their use of ingredients, their distilling location and process, bottling location and process, and aging process.*

The American rum distilling movement started in the '90s with just a handful of craft producers and has now grown to well over 250 distilleries.[13]

When she started, one of the befriended distillers, Todd Leopold, convinced Maggie to enroll at the Siebel Institute of Technology, one of the top brewing and distilling educators in the United States. "As a young woman, having a piece of paper that proved I knew what I was doing was important," she explains. "I don't know if I could have had my career otherwise."

But despite her background and practical know-how, it was hard for Maggie to be taken seriously. "In the United States, the typical caricature of a distiller is an old white guy in overalls," she laughs. A female distiller was not welcome in the spirits world, but Maggie was determined to prove herself.

She reached out to different distilleries in search of experience. "At the time, there was not much information online, especially not in English. So, I emailed a well-respected brandy producer, Germain-Robin, saying I'd like to learn about traditional cognac methods." After a few exchanges, Maggie was on a plane to California to join the company as an assistant distiller.

---

13 Source: https://www.americanrumreport.com/distillery-index

Maggie checks in on production in her overalls.

Her cognac adventure taught her valuable skills such as aging and blending. She also got to taste a lot of old spirits: "I've been fortunate enough to taste liquids from different stills, distilled in different ways, with different terms of aging," she recalls. "I got to learn a lot. It was a formative experience for me."

Todd Leopold was a supportive figure throughout Maggie's career. He advised her to work in distribution, the part of the business distillers overlook. "It's all about the life of your product after it leaves your hands. And it's so important to know how that all works," she explains.

With the complex legal systems that many US distillers face, understanding how the spirits live out in the real world gave Maggie a commercial edge. With all that experience, Maggie felt ready to open a rye whiskey distillery.

One day, she got a phone call from Privateer Rum in Ipswich, Massachusetts. "It was actually Hubert from Germain-Robin who met the owner of Privateer. They wanted to make fine quality rum, and they needed someone very picky, quality-oriented, and demanding," she recalls. "Hubert recommended me and convinced me to take the job."

At Privateer Rum, Maggie extracts a small portion of rum out of a barrel for sampling.

Although this wasn't part of her plan, Maggie took the opportunity and became the company's master distiller and blender. "I always joke that I didn't pick rum; rum picked me," she laughs. "I got sucked into this new world, and I don't think I'll ever want to leave."

"It's all about the life of your product after it leaves your hands."

Since joining in 2012, Maggie positioned Privateer as one of the leading American craft rum producers. "I believe rum can be just as sophisticated as wine. I strive to make it consistently better," she explains.

After almost a decade of developing the brand, Maggie departed from Privateer in January 2021, with a view of starting her own venture. As we're talking, Maggie's desk is full of samples from three different countries and multiple distilleries.

"People keep asking me to taste their product and help them develop their spirits with them. I get to live out my dream as a blender," she smiles. On October 1st, 2021, Maggie joined Mount Gay as their new

Estate Rum Manager. She will oversee the entire lifecycle of the new estate rum division and work alongside Trudiann Branker.

Of course, as a female distiller, her dreams were often covered with doubts. In one instance, she was refused a job because she was female. "My tutor and mentor reassured me it had nothing to do with my lack of skills," she explains. "They believed in me and told me I was ready to run my own distillery."

"I always joke that I didn't pick rum; rum picked me."

Reflecting on how these challenges affected her career, she echoes thought female leaders are all too familiar with: "I really thought that I wasn't good enough, or I didn't have what it took. I could study and work hard, but I still believed I wasn't worthy. Imagine what my career would be like if I were a man who didn't have to deal with these doubts or undermining comments."

She adds that a lot of negative experiences result from internalized sexism. "It's the little things that can become the shoelace that snaps, like in that poem by Charles Bukowski," she explains. "For instance, one time I had to arrange a permit over the phone, and I could hear the person started to treat me differently once he realized I was a woman. It's the 'little tragedies' that eventually drive you crazy."

The rum industry has a lot of broken shoelaces, and it's not always safe and welcoming for women. "So much business is discussed at events, at the bar late at night. That's when you bond," she explains. "Once it gets past 10:00 p.m., I no longer feel safe," she tells us. "Men can enjoy the evening and focus on developing business relationships, while half of my brain is in a whole different universe. I have to stay alert, refuse drinks without being rude, and figure out how to get back to the hotel safely."

Most professional women can relate to these inequalities, which are particularly evident in the spirits industry. One of her biggest influences, Karen Hoskin of Montanya Distillers, often supported her during difficult times. "She's one of the very first people I called to ask, 'What should I do next?' " Maggie adds later, "She's been in the scene for a long time and had to deal with the same things."

As we see more prominent figures like Karen and organizations hiring more women in key roles, it's important to recall Maggie's belief in personal development. As companies promote inclusivity and diversity, it's important they develop a culture of belonging.

"If you have not made your organization a place where women can succeed, you're putting those people in harm's way," she reflects. "Hiring female executives is not enough if they will be treated badly. There needs to be actual effort rather than gestures."

Boulevardier

"This is initially a whiskey cocktail made with bourbon. I usually drink my rum straight—a bottle of rum with two glasses, a friend, and a good conversation. But as a cocktail, I have to pick the Rum Boulevardier. One of my local places calls this order a 'Killjoy' after me. It's a long story..."

—Maggie

Glass: Rocks
Garnish: Orange peel

1½ oz. Mount Gay Black Barrel Rum
1 oz. Campari
1 oz. sweet vermouth

Add all ingredients to a mixing glass and stir with ice. Strain over clean ice into a rocks glass.

Kayla's Tip:
Choosing the right sweet vermouth is key. I recommend starting with favorites like Antica Formula, Cocchi del Torino, or Punt e Mes. Be sure to branch out and try small-batch sweet vermouths, dry or blanc vermouths, or another kind of fortified wine.

Good to Know:
Once a bottle of vermouth is opened, store it in the fridge or it will spoil! Even then, you have a couple of months, so try and keep your bottles small.

Chapter 16

Maria Izabel Costa, Cachaça Maria Izabel, Brazil

Before introducing our next master blender, we must come clean: she is not really a rum maker, at least not in a traditional sense. Maria Izabel Costa produces cachaça (pronounced ka-sha-sa), a Brazilian spirit made of fermented sugarcane juice. While it's like rum in many ways, there are some production differences, such as using various types of wood that give cachaça its typical, grassy taste. Still, we simply couldn't overlook Maria's story—the fearless, barefoot lady who followed her dreams and single-handedly set up a distillery in the middle of nowhere.

Maria was born in Paraty, a picturesque town on the Atlantic coast of Brazil. She grew up on an old cachaça farm that belonged to her paternal ancestors. Her father passed away when she was only four years old, discontinuing production and stopping the family business.

Still, the cachaça tradition must have stayed in the back of Maria's mind. She was surrounded by what could have been, raised by the hard-working women in her family. "The female figure has always been very striking in my life as I was nurtured by my mother, maternal aunts, and my Lebanese grandmother," she explains.

Cachaça was part of Maria's family since the nineteenth century. Some of the earliest documents confirm that her great-grandfather produced this spirit on three farms and even gifted his special reserve to King Albert I of Belgium. Then, Maria's grandfather, also one of the most important mayors of Paraty, continued the production until the 1940s. With Maria's father dying so young, it seemed like the family business was a thing of the past. Many years later, she would resume production under her name, though it wasn't always an obvious career path.

A statue of King Albert I of Belgium, who was gifted a special cachaça reserve by Maria's great-grandfather.

Maria always felt a special connection to nature, and it is safe to say that Mother Earth was another significant "female" influence in her life. Maria spent her formative years between her family's farm and the historic center of Paraty. This combination gave her the best of both worlds, growing up surrounded by Brazil's breathtaking flora and her favorite seaside nearby. Later, she escaped deep into the forest on the edge of Paraty Bay, where she still lives today.

If you were to meet Maria, you'd think she's the incarnation of beautiful Mother Nature herself. You'd also be lucky to see her wearing shoes. She rejects them out of deep respect for her surroundings: "I walk on earth as I walk in my house, barefoot," she tells us. "As a little girl, I only wore shoes in places where I couldn't go barefoot, such as school, public offices, or the church. Shoes always hindered me when it came to climbing trees, walking into waterfalls, entering the waters of rivers and the sea. I currently only use them for travel. Perhaps that's why I travel very little," she laughs.

Maria had no academic training as she entered adulthood early, and life didn't spare her from personal tragedies. She got married at the age of seventeen and had five daughters with her first husband. Unfortunately, one of them only lived a few months, which was a heartbreaking event. Later, she had her sixth daughter, Maia, who was born with Down Syndrome. "She required special care, which is why I didn't start producing cachaça until 1996," she tells us. Maria always did her best to provide for all her daughters, using, as she says, the best, given her circumstances.

Maria had no time for formal education between helping her husband with his work and taking care of her girls. "I had no profession, so I started to plant more vegetables than we needed and sell the surplus," she explains. "I also sold homemade bread and jam, which I made at night while my daughters slept."

She later took the opportunity to sew fabric bikinis for stores in the area. These were fashionable at the time, and it was an honest way to make an extra income while taking care of her children. "I started to earn a little more when I decided to work with ornamental plants and take care of gardens," she recalls.

Although she lived at the edge of the river Encachoeirado, she needed the wild seawaters the most. "I bought a motorized canoe, and on the weekends, I would go to the islands of Paraty with my daughters," she recalls. "Once I got there, a new universe opened up to me. I made friends, I participated in a theater group, and everything seemed to flow."

Maria sits outside in the company of her five children.

At the time, she was experiencing some personal turbulences, leading her to remarry her ex-husband. But when her fifth daughter was born, she had the courage to leave for good. "I was no longer afraid of the challenges of survival on my own," she tells us. "I wanted more space. I wanted to plant trees, have animals, take care of my horses, and be more inserted in nature."

As she became a single mother with freshly found independence, Maria could finally live according to her values.

After the final separation from her husband, she used her savings to buy the site at Sítio Santo Antônio, where the distillery now operates. This picturesque place was only reachable by boat or foot back then, but that didn't stop her. "I arrived there in the 1980s, with not much money," she recalls. "There was no electricity until 2009, nor access by car to the site." Still, she fell in love with her surroundings, which many visitors describe as an unspoiled paradise.

"I was no longer afraid of the challenges of survival on my own. I wanted more space. I wanted to plant trees, have animals, take care of my horses, and be more inserted in nature."

Maria makes a trip through the Encachoeirado river.

The property was in poor condition, so she sold part of the land to make it livable. Maria tells us this was a period of hard work, especially since she was also a tourist guide on the weekends—a job that required a long boat trip to Paraty. The repaired farm is also where her sixth daughter was born in 1994 when she set up the still.

Although making cachaça was part of her family DNA, Maria claims the decision to start producing was a mere consequence of circumstances. "I always wanted to live close to nature," she says. "With no electricity and no road, there was not much I could do." Later, she adds, "One day, as I was passing by the highway, I saw some gentlemen cutting sugarcane. I asked them to keep the tips for me so I could plant them on the farm. I bagged the remains of the cane and transported it to the site in a rowing canoe."

Maria planted the sugarcane field all by herself. It grows easily, and the microclimate seemed perfect for cachaça, which gave her the idea to set up a still. But how to overcome the lack of electricity? "I took advantage of the slope of the land, so gravity did its job. To grind the cane, I used a diesel engine," she explains.

With all machinery installed, she finally became an independent producer with her own label, *Cachaça Maria Izabel*.

Maria bottles her cachaça and adds the finishing touches.

In the beginning, Maria's distillery was a one-woman operation. She'd go from bar to bar trying to sell her cachaça, which was difficult as you never see women making and selling this spirit in Brazil. "I suffered a lot of prejudice and got mean comments from the men. I didn't pay much attention to that. I believe that the challenges can only make us stronger," she recalls.

Eventually, her cachaça gained appreciation in Paraty and beyond, becoming one of the most renowned brands in Brazil. Still, she keeps her production small, limited to the sugarcane that grows on her property. "For me, it is essential that the cane is organic and processed immediately after cutting," she explains. This way, her cachaça has the lowest acidity index in the area. "We do not use any chemical additives. We work as one organism. The land is alive, and we respect it. Our production is part of a lifestyle, not a business."

Maria has since hired three collaborators, all flexible in their tasks. Some work in the field but also help with general services. One of her daughters takes care of the office and welcomes tourists. During harvest, she hires one more person to help cut the sugarcane. Everything is kept low-key and very traditional. "I am known as 'the last of the Moícanas' because I still grind the cane manually," she laughs. "In distillation, one employee replaces me when necessary. As for standardization, bottling, and labeling, I'm still the only one doing it." She also uses artisan baking yeast for fermentation, which she prepares according to a late nineteenth-century recipe.

"The land is alive, and we respect it. Our production is part of a lifestyle, not a business."

Maria puts a lot of love and attention into her product. Her motto is to take great care of each stage of the process as if it were the most important one. "My pride is the result of a job well done," she tells us. "The world of cachaça is vast, and I'm just a small producer. I do things my way, a feminine way; that's what I am."

Her greatest achievement is that she stayed faithful to her personal beliefs, a lesson she'd like to pass on to future generations of female distillers. "May the girls follow the paths they choose, respecting their values."

Indeed, despite her success, Maria stays humble and committed to working as one with nature. Now and then, she gets business proposals, which she declines, as she's content with her current life. "You can't ride on two horses simultaneously; you will fall. Having more money only gives more problems," she smiles. "Right now, I am where I want to be. Everything is great; it is really great."

Cai Tai

"I don't like cocktails; they are too sweet for me. I only drink pure cachaça and, of course, one that I make. But I noticed that the Thai Brazil restaurant Prosa na Praça in nearby Paraty makes several cocktails with my brand in it. From what I heard, this is a popular one; for sure, it is aromatic."

—Maria

Glass: Wine
Garnish: A slice of star fruit and spring flower

1½ oz. Maria Izabel
6 lychees
½ oz. Demerara syrup
¾ oz. lemon juice
12 ice cubes

Add all ingredients to a blender. The higher the speed, the creamier. Pour into a wine glass.

Kayla's Tip:
You can easily add depth and complexity to this cocktail. Although the original recipe called for lychee syrup, try substituting it with demerara, orgeat (my top pick!), honey, agave, or even maple syrup.

DIY Tip:
To make demerara syrup, heat equal parts demerara sugar and water until the sugar dissolves.

Chapter 17

Chantal Comte, Rhum Chantal Comte, France

Today, consumers are increasingly aware of rum as a sipping drink with rich complexity and style. However, this wasn't always the case. Back in the 1980s, the rum industry was experiencing an all-time low. Producers could not sell their stock, and the general perception was that rum was far from elegant.

"Madam, we do not buy drinks for dockers" is a sentence that Chantal Comte heard all too often, yet it didn't stop her from spreading her rum gospel and raising awareness of this noble spirit. In 1983, she became an independent bottler, and today, her brand *Rhum Chantal Comte* is synonymous with luxury and prestige.

Chantal was born in colorful Casablanca, Morocco. The place might not be known for its rum—or alcohol, for that matter—but it's full of vibrant flavors and spices that influenced Chantal's nose growing up. Her family had a garden with flowers and herbs, which she learned to recognize by smell. "It prepared me for my current job. I still search for beautiful aromas I remember from that time when I create new blends," she tells us.

Chantal was so fascinated with the power of scent, and during her time as a schoolteacher, she taught kids to use their noses and recognize different smells in products like cola. "Unfortunately, the school asked me to stop, as several parents worried that this would drive them toward alcohol. I think the nose is often a taboo in our society."

France was a second home to Chantal as her family had a wine estate in Costières-de-Nîmes, southern Rhône (called Château de la Tuilerie). As she tells us, her father encouraged her to take risks in life. Perhaps that's why—despite having a "safe" career as a winegrower—Chantal jumped into the world of rum at a time nobody else did.

An early photograph of Chantal.

Her father wasn't optimistic about the future of wine in the area and even considered selling the vineyard before Chantal took it over. "I convinced him to keep it. I believed our terroir and production methods had a future," she explains.

Time proved she was right, though she recalls it was nothing more than a gamble. "I had a lot of innocence then since I didn't know anything about wine and, frankly, didn't even drink it," she laughs. But she quickly understood that she had to know the product well to be taken seriously in her niche.

One day, she worked at a wine fair in France when some customers approached her with questions. "A group of men came up to my booth and asked about the wine I represented. I wasn't sure of the grape variety, so they laughed at me," she recalls. "I shut the booth and decided to talk to the other wine producers at the event and learn all about what they were doing. That's when I got genuinely fascinated by the job."

Soon after, she was determined to take over the family business, studying and learning practical winemaking skills at the Château. "It was a fantastic time of my life. I had no past obligations and an open future where everything was possible. I was free to do what I thought was right," she tells us.

Her father's car distribution business led Chantal to Martinique, where she first fell in love with rum. She didn't care much about cars, so she spent her time touring around the island and visiting rum distilleries. "I couldn't even recognize my own vehicle if it was standing in front of me, so I found something else to do," she laughs. "Rum fascinated me, but in those years, the producers sold almost nothing. Even when you went to someone's house, they would offer you whisky rather than rum. They were not proud of their products. It struck me a lot."

Over time, she discovered rum could be just as complex and sophisticated as wine, and she wanted to learn everything about *rhum agricole*. She befriended André Depaz, a renowned distiller in Martinique, who taught her a lot about the spirit.

"I learned how to recognize high-quality rum and make blends," she tells us. "I also understood that one product could not be imitated at a different location. People can try to make the same rum in South America or another country; they will not succeed in it."

To this day, she remains faithful to the rums of Martinique and has developed excellent sensory skills through her years of practice. "I drink very little; each drop must be tasted like a treasure," she tells us. "One drop is enough for me to have all the information I need, so my palate is not damaged by violent tastings."

A very elegant Chantal attends an event.

She credits Depaz for inspiring her to become an independent blender and bottler in 1983, a profession that existed in whisky but was unheard of in rum. He entrusted her with one of his best rums, vintage 1975, which, to this day, remains highly sought after by rum enthusiasts and collectors.

"I was not a distiller; I only selected exceptional cuvées under the brand that I created," she explains. "I created my own job and became the first independent female rum blender." Later, she adds: "I went into this business against everyone's advice, at a time of a huge slump for many rum producers. It was the passion for an abused and unrecognized product that drove me to do it. I followed my instincts, convinced that rum would enter the court of great spirits one day. The future proved me right, but I had to wait twenty years!"

Indeed, *Rhum Chantal Comte* steadily gained recognition among connoisseurs, and eventually, she gave up her wine business entirely.

Chantal's first-ever bottling (under her label), contained Depaz rum from 1975, considered a "classical year" for *rhum agricole*. René van Hoven, coauthor of this book, is lucky to have this rare (as of 2021, yet unopened) gem in his vintage rum collection. He also tasted it at an event years ago and can attest to its excellent character.

Chantal is very strict when it comes to selecting her spirits, and the quality of the environment plays a crucial role. Indeed, there are many elements to consider when creating rum—the forest, climate, humidity, terroir, and countless other things make the final liquid unique.

"One drop is enough for me to have all the information I need, so my palate is not damaged by violent tastings."

Chantal loves to soak up the atmosphere of the place during tastings and believes nature can be found on the palate. As she tells us, she once rejected a business opportunity in Japan for this reason. "The distillery was located in a polluted area full of smog. How could a product like that be of high quality?" she reflects. That's why protecting the environment is vital for Chantal. She proudly supports the Caribaea Initiative, an organization which trains young scientists in the West Indies to preserve biodiversity on the islands.

Caribaea Initiative is the only international nature-conservation organization undertaking actions covering all the Caribbean islands, regardless of linguistic, cultural, or political barriers. The Caribbean islands are one of the most biodiverse sites in the world but are also among the areas most exposed to the consequences of climate change.

Since nobody believed rum could be a premium spirit back then, it was a long and frustrating battle, which Chantal was determined to win. "For twenty years, I preached about rum and worked hard to grow its popularity among consumers. And for a long time, I encountered polite refusals," she tells us.

When asked if being a woman in the spirits world ever hindered her efforts, she states: "I never asked myself the question of whether I was legitimate in this male world. No one told me it was impossible, so I did it with complete innocence."

Chantal thinks women have an edge when it comes to tasting and smelling, so they can become excellent blenders with some training and practice. "We are capable of detecting things because it's usually women who cook; it's women who give birth to children and feel whether their babies are sick. We have a wild instinct and use our noses more often than men," she says.

However, she feels many women do not feel welcome in the spirits world because alcoholic drinks are typically marketed to men. "In my winemaking days, I often saw couples arriving to visit the cellar. However, only men got out while women stayed in the car. I thought that it was unacceptable, so I rearranged my cellar to make it appealing in the eyes of women, too. And it worked. They felt more comfortable, listened to what was going on during the tastings, and were very interested."

Still, she rejects the notion that being female ever stopped her from pursuing her career as an independent rum blender. "I never paid attention to negativity. Maybe because I was a woman winegrower at a time when there were not many of us," she tells us. "There are so many remarkable women who changed the world with their determination. Look at Alexandra David-Neel, who climbed the Himalayas at ninety-six years old, Helene Boucher, the first woman pilot in the 1930s, or Indira Gandhi, who was elected prime minister in India. They followed their paths no matter what others thought. I'm not saying I'm a heroine like these great women, but I do not want to think of myself as a victim of sexism."

"I never asked myself the question of whether I was legitimate in this male world. No one told me it was impossible, so I did it with complete innocence."

Her persistence is evident in her work, as not only did she pursue rum against everyone's advice, but she also aimed for perfection each time. "I am fortunate to have a nose and palate that work rather well, so I cannot accept having something average. I don't want to go to great lengths for something that will be *just* good. I need excellence."

Chantal visits her family's wine estate, Château de la Tuilerie, in southern Rhône.

ClubHouse

"This is the best way to overcome a heatwave. The drink is as blue as the pool, and I presented this one on Instagram two years ago. Recently I noticed that several bars served it, and I was very proud of that. It's fresh, nicely colored, and fun to drink. I am sure some dry champagne will be a nice finish as well."

—Chantal

Glass: Highball
Garnish: A lime wedge and mint sprig

2 oz. Fighting Spirit Gold
½ oz. Blue Curaçao
¾ oz. lime
Splash of soda water

Add all ingredients to a mixing glass, shake with ice, and strain over ice into a glass. Top with soda water.

Kayla's Tip:
The original recipe called for either soda or bay water, but soda water is probably easier to find. If you are in a luxurious mood, try topping with dry champagne instead.

DIY Tip:
When preparing your garnish, use the top part of your mint to create a bushy bouquet. Lightly slap the mint on the back of your hand to unlock those refreshing, minty smells.

Chapter 18

Trudiann Branker, Mount Gay, Barbados

We couldn't skip Trudiann Branker of Mount Gay in Barbados, who unfortunately couldn't join this project. The history of rum as we know it today started in Barbados, and we feel the book would be incomplete without her.

Working for the oldest rum company in the world, Trudiann is a part of the new generation of master blenders. She joined Mount Gay in 2014 as a graduate of Howard University and started as the quality assurance manager. In April 2019, she officially replaced her mentor, Allen Smith, and became the first female master blender of Mount Gay Rum. She was the first woman in the history of the entire island to hold that recognition.

As soon as she started her new position, she took the lead on resetting the brand while also keeping a keen eye on Mount Gay's three-hundred-year-old tradition. Refining their premium portfolio with new techniques, she also accomplished a more transparent way of working in the rum industry.

We're told that Trudiann loves walking through the warehouses, looking at all the barrels, and smelling the aging liquids.

Chapter 19

Renegade Rum

This book features sixteen (plus one) amazing women recounting their journeys as master blenders. However, this picture is far from complete. The number of women in the rum industry is growing, not just in the world of blending. New opportunities are opening across all levels and departments.

Here are only some of the jobs that the industry can offer: sales or export manager, bartender or mixologist, blogger or journalist, public relations or marketing coordinator, brand ambassador or manager, production planner...or perhaps a distillery owner?

As several experts noted, there is a new generation of female rum blenders in training. For some companies, it's a conscious choice, as the feminine element is desirable in their rum; for others, it's a selection based on skills alone. The aforementioned "feminine element" is, of course, impossible to define as it's so subjective. We like to think of it as smooth, elegant, complex, and nuanced.

Let's meet a group of women who are part of a new brand in Grenada, the Caribbean, bearing a fitting name: Renegade Rum.

Renegade's distillation team—Karla Harford, Camille Charles, Devon Date, Kerissa Briggs, and Ainka Hastick—chat with two other staff members.

Breaking old macho traditions may be hard in established companies, but new brands can look at their production needs and hire the best staff to fulfill them. Renegade is a fine example of such a company. They started their first distillation on a sunny September afternoon in 2020, and they're already highly committed to keeping their environment clean, boosting the island's economy, and providing a transparent, traceable, and sustainable product. With only qualified staff from the local community, the current master distiller and blender (or head distiller, in their terminology) is Devon Date, who previously developed his skills at Clarke's Court Distillery. He is also responsible for mentoring four women—Karla, Ainka, Camille, Kerissa—who will become future master blenders (or head blenders, to use their preferred term).

All his trainees have backgrounds in engineering or chemistry, and the company insists they were chosen because they were the best candidates for the job. Renegade also employs women in other areas of the company. We're told that most applications come from women, and while there was never an official quota to meet, Renegade is proud to bring opportunities to the talented and hard-working women of Grenada.

Renegade's CEO, Mark Reynier, is very aware of his role in removing the limitations for women in the spirits industry. After all, gender inclusivity is not just a women's issue. He is no stranger to the distilling business and is adamant that companies need to make more effort to attract and hire female employees. Maybe it's time to change the terminology— *head blender* attests to the team effort behind blending and abandons masculine connotations associated with the term *master blender.*

Without further ado, let's meet Renegade's up and coming female distilling team:

Karla

Since 2016, Karla Harford has been thriving in the manufacturing industry. Her introduction to the field began early that year when Coca-Cola Grenada hired her as their integrated systems coordinator. From there on, she realized she had a real knack in the manufacturing industry. "Though a distillery was never part of my foreseen plan, the experience and knowledge obtained here have been truly remarkable."

Ainka

Before her employment at the distillery, Ainka Hastick was an undergraduate student. She fell in love with the chemistry and biological science of producing rum; it captured her and got her involved.

"My favorite part of the job is the 'metamorphosis' of spirit production, and an important lesson I've learned thus far is the importance of patience."

Camille

A science teacher and physiology and molecular biology tutor, Camille
Charles' favorite part of the job is nosing the spirit and knowing when to
make her "cuts." This means she enjoys the responsibility to choose the
distillation part used in the final rum.

"I like being able to apply scientific principles to the distillation process."

> In distillation, fresh spirits consist of three "parts": the head, the
> heart, and the tail. The heart is the desirable part of the rum, and
> the rest goes into the next distillation stage. The head can give
> headaches and the tail is watery, so distillers need to know when to
> "cut." The cut is the moment where the distiller decides where one
> part ends and the other part starts.

Kerissa

Before joining Renegade Rum, Kerissa Briggs worked at another
distillery as a lab technician. She was excited to be part of the actual
manufacturing of the spirit. Having moved from an older distillery to a
newer one, Kerissa says:

"I really appreciate how modernized a lot of the processes are in terms of
the level of automation and digitization implemented in the operations."

A Final Note

While the spirits industry is becoming more female-friendly, bringing more women into the existing rum world is not as easy as it sounds. There is still a lack of awareness that representation matters, and that diversity can benefit any company. Younger women and girls may feel encouraged to pursue certain roles if they see a female doing the job. Similarly, joining an all-male company might feel threatening or uncomfortable, so companies should make efforts to treat all employees fairly and put effective bullying and sexual harassment policies in place. Sadly, several women we've interviewed experienced inappropriate behavior from their male peers on various occasions, and out of concern for their safety, we agreed not to disclose some details.

Sexual harassment is still a sad reality for many professional women, not just in the spirits industry. The working environment should be a place where women feel accepted, valued, and safe. It's not just the leadership that needs to change, but also the behavior of the coworkers. So educate your staff, encourage sensitivity training, and nurture everyone's unique skills. There's a lot of research suggesting that diverse companies with female leadership can thrive and generate extra market value, so sticking to the old-fashioned gender bias is hurtful and counterproductive. For the same reason, we hope female business owners will be able to access the same capital as their male colleagues as the spirits world needs more diverse flavors and more female-led distilleries.

Lastly, equal access to education is essential if we want more women to join this field. Being a master blender calls for highly technical skills and a chemistry or biotechnology background, so we need to encourage girls to pursue STEM disciplines and not limit their full potential. As we've learned from several stories in this book, education and positive mentorship are hugely important. We remain hopeful that with recent calls to bring more girls to science, female mentorship and funding initiatives undertaken by some of our Rum Rebels, and emerging women champions like Renegade, the rum industry will continue changing for the better. And rest assured, the cliche male, rum-drinking pirate stereotype will soon fade away like a ghostship on the horizon.

PS. We sincerely hope that you've enjoyed reading this book as much as we've enjoyed writing it. We'd love to connect with other rum fans and badass female alcohol makers, so don't hesitate to drop us a line at hello@tripsandtaste.com (also, make sure to follow Trips & Taste on Facebook and @RenesRarities on Instagram). Last but not least, we'd appreciate a review on Amazon to help us spread the word about our fearless *Rum Rebels* and their amazing contributions to the spirits industry and their communities.

Acknowledgments

First of all, we want to thank Jessica Faroy (Mango Publishing) for contacting us. Without that first contact, this book wouldn't exist.

We'd also like to thank Kayla Cross, Roelof Gorissen, and Charley Rousset, thanks to whom you can recreate and enjoy all the delicious cocktails in this book!

We'd also like to thank the following for helping us reach all our amazing *Rum Rebels*:

- J. Wray and Nephew Limited/Campari Group: Erin Smolinski, Alison Moss-Solomon
- Zacapa/Diageo: Sara Playá Cavallé
- Destileria Carúpano C.A., Ana Elena Rubino
- Depaz, Dillon, Benoit Bail-Danel
- Casa Tarasco
- Angostura Limited, Sharda Boodram, Judy Kanhai
- Montanya Distillers, Jenny Foust
- Botran, Oscar Mendez
- Brugal, Pavol Kazimir
- J.M, Marie Olona, Audrey Bruisson, Emmanuel Becheau
- Demerara Distillers Limited
- Corporación Cuba Ron S.A., Claudia Montes de Oca Rivas
- Don Q, Serralles, Yisell Muxo
- Maggie Campbell
- Maria Izabel, Mariza Izabel, Leszek Wedzich
- Chantal Comte
- Mount Gay/Remy Martin, Julie Padovani

- Renegade Rum Distillery, Mark Newton
- Liz Palmer, UPSocial Wine & Spirits
- Federico J. Hernandez (Women Leading Rum)
- Kris Von Stedingk

And finally, huge thanks to the entire team at Mango Publishing for all their work and patience.

During the creation of our book, we have relied on the research and expertise of the following sources:

- Dr. Paul Breslin: professor at the department of nutritional sciences at Rutgers University and a researcher at the Monell Chemical Senses Center
- Institute of Biomedical Sciences: at the Federal University of Rio de Janeiro in Brazil
- Rich Michaels: quality and innovation manager at FX Matt Brewing and a brewing instructor at Schenectady County Community College
- Deborah Parker: prevention.com
- Neil Martin: Director of the Human Olfaction Laboratory at Middlesex University
- Linda May Bartoshuk: Psychologist, Yale University (linda.bartoshuk@yale.edu)
- Kathrin Ohla and Johan Lundstrom: Monell Chemical Senses Center and the Department of Clinical Neuroscience Karolinska Institutet, Stockholm
- Federal University of Rio de Janeiro
- University of São Paulo
- University of California–San Francisco
- University of Copenhagen
- National Institute on Deafness and Other Communication

Disorders (NIDCD): Statistics on Taste

- National Library of Medicine: PTC/PROP tasting
- The University of Nottingham
- The National Archives Museum: Spirited Republic: Alcohol in American History
- JSTOR Alcohol Consumption During Prohibition
- Alcohol Problems and Solutions
- *Harvard Business Review*
- Minnesota Women's Press
- *Medical News Today*
- Psych Manics

About the Authors

Martyna Halas

Born and raised in Bydgoszcz, Poland, Martyna has lived in Germany, Ireland, and the Netherlands. She has contributed to various international blogs and magazines like HealthyPlace.com or *Are We Europe* and currently works as a freelance journalist and content creator. She is also a singer collaborating with multiple artists in the rock and metal scene and the front lady of Ascend the Hollow and Rage of Light. She's a passionate advocate for mental health, women's reproductive rights, and gender diversity in music and beyond. Privately, she enjoys craft beer and can't skip a city without checking some locally made specialties. Her interest in rum grew when she met René van Hoven, with whom she launched a website, TripsAndTaste.com, and traveled to several spirits events such as the German Rum Festival in Berlin or Michelangelo International Wine and Spirits Awards in South Africa. Her goal is to break the stereotypes about women and rum and bring well-deserved attention to female-led distilleries.

René van Hoven

Born and raised just north of Amsterdam, René is an F&B (food and beverage) teacher, international wine and spirits judge, and vintage rum collector (known online as René's Rarities). As a chef and wine and spirits specialist, he has always worked with flavors and loves to write about them. He has contributed articles to newspapers and international magazines such as *More Than Drinks*, *Whisky Passion*, *Rum Porter*, and many more. He is a recurring guest at various European spirits festivals like the German Rum Festival Berlin, Brau Beviale in Nuernberg, Salon du Rhum Belgique in Spa, and Rhum Fest Paris. He often gives masterclasses at various events to share his knowledge about rum and its history. When traveling to festivals, he brings a selection of his private vintage bottles to share with other rum enthusiasts.

Meet the Mixologist

Amsterdam-based mixologist Kayla Cross is the owner of The Little White Bird cocktail pub. Originating from Los Angeles, she started her bartending career in New Orleans. As she loves to travel, she has lived and worked in six countries and crossed four continents. Eventually, she started her own hospitality management and consulting business and assisted in new venue launches several times. This experience inspired her to create a place of her own with her experienced and talented partner Roelof Gorissen. Together, they opened a cocktail pub in the beautiful historic farmers' market, the Albert Cuyp, in Amsterdam, the Netherlands.

The Little White Bird opened in late January 2020, and as Kayla tells us, it has been the biggest challenge of her career by far. She and her partner built the place with their own hands. The phenomenal bar team continued to be flexible and relentless as they tackled the ever-constant curveballs the pandemic has thrown their way. Her team is part of the stellar local community that has lifted it all, despite the unfortunate timing of the grand opening.

The pub's name is a nod to the famous literary character, Peter Pan. The character was first mentioned in a play entitled "The Little White Bird," part of Kayla's and Roelof's charming love story. As it turns out, they both used Peter Pan as a nickname way before they first met. The core of the bar's concept is marrying high-end drinks with the warm atmosphere of the Irish pub culture, where Kayla and Roelof met. Many Irish pub names often include a color or an animal, which is why The Little White Bird's logo is a heron. But we recommend our readers to visit the bar themselves, have a drink, and let the owners tell their full story; it sounds much better then!

Kayla's top secret tips to remember at all times when you are making your cocktails:

- Always use fresh juice when possible
- Always taste your drink after creation and before pouring it into your chilled cocktail glass so you can adjust accordingly
- Too sour? Add a bar spoon of sugar
- Too sweet? Add a bar spoon of citrus
- Missing that punch or sparkle? Add a bar spoon of rum
- Best is to add in small amounts; it is easier to add extra than to take out what's already in

The Little White Bird cocktail menu is hyper-seasonal. Kayla and Roelef use fresh produce from the market in front of their door and interpret it across seven flavor profiles: boozy, bitter, sweet, sour, wild card, classic, and alco free/light. This way, they make sure to utilize every part of the ingredients differently for each unique drink. Once the market runs out of a seasonal component, Kayla moves on to the next recipe. This makes each menu last for about two weeks, making it ideal for the team to challenge their creativity constantly and for the visitors to taste something new each time. For instance, Kayla and Roelof's close-knit bar birds get to try exciting things like the watermelon rind kimchi, house-made Dutch chocolate mole, or lacto-fermented okra rapid-infused jenever. And before you say that fast ten times, go to the bar to have a drink first—it might help!

Finally, the true cocktail nerds among our readers will appreciate not just the liquid but also the glass that comes with the drink. As Kayla likes to joke, she has a true glass fetish, and she insists: "It's such an underrated part of cocktails, but so crucial!" Make sure to check out what the bar has to offer on that front, and you'll probably agree with that statement.

Although The Little White Bird has not been open long due to COVID-19 (a total of three months as we're writing this chapter), it has already received notable awards and recognitions, such as:

- Top 5 best new bars in Amsterdam;
- Best old-fashioned cocktail in the Netherlands (*Esquire* magazine);
- Extensive feature in *Entree* magazine;
- Two team members named top fifteen in World Class Netherlands 2020;
- One team member named Nikka Netherlands Cocktail champion;
- One team member named Chivas Global Cocktail champion;
- Feature in *Bittered Sling* magazine (a project entitled "Leadership in Our Community").

The Little White Bird roosts at:
159 Albert Cuypstraat in Amsterdam, the Netherlands
www.thelittlewhitebirdams.com

Photo Credits

Foreword:

Liz Palmer

Intro:

Zacapa/Diageo
Dmitry Pichugin (stock.adobe.com)

Chapter 1:

Metropolitan Museum of NYC
Hieronymus Brunschwig, 1512
Pictolic.com
Daily Mirror (https://artsandculture.google.com)

Chapters 2–19:

Joy Spence: J. Wray and Nephew: Limited / Campari Group
Lorena Vásquez Ampié: Zacapa / Diageo
Carmen López de Bastidas: Destileria Carúpano C.A.
Stéphanie Dufour: Depaz/Dillon
Miriam Paola Pacheco: Casa Tarasco
Carol Homer-Caesar: Angostura Limited
Karen Hoskin: Montanya Distillers
Magda López: Botran
Jassil Villanueva: Brugal
Karine Lassalle: Rhum J.M
Sharon Baksh: Demerara Distillers Limited
Salomé Alemán: Corporación Cuba Ron S.A.
Silvia Santiago: Don Q, Serralles

Maggie Campbell: Maggie Campbell / Privateer Rum Distillery
Maria Izabel: Maria Izabel
Chantal Comte: Chantal Comte
Trudiann Branker: Mount Gay / Remy Martin
Renegade Rum: Renegade Rum distillery

Meet the Mixologist:

Kayla Cross: Marek Brychcy

Cocktails:

Charley Rousset (www.charley.vision)

yellow pear 🍐 press

Yellow Pear Press, established in 2015, publishes inspiring, charming, clever, distinctive, playful, imaginative, beautifully designed lifestyle books, cookbooks, literary fiction, notecards, and journals with a certain *joie de vivre* in both content and style. Yellow Pear Press books have been honored by the Independent Publisher Book (IPPY) Awards, National Indie Excellence Awards, Independent Press Awards, and International Book Awards. Reviews of our titles have appeared in Kirkus Reviews, Foreword Reviews, Booklist, Midwest Book Review, San Francisco Chronicle, and New York Journal of Books, among others. Yellow Pear Press joined forces with Mango Publishing in 2020, both with the vision to continue publishing clever and innovative books. The fact that they're both named after fruit is a total coincidence.

We love hearing from our readers, so please stay in touch with us and follow us at:

Facebook: Mango Publishing
Twitter: @MangoPublishing
Instagram: @MangoPublishing
LinkedIn: Mango Publishing
Pinterest: Mango Publishing
Newsletter: mangopublishinggroup.com/newsletter